T0328475

Cambridge Elements ☰

Elements in the Philosophy of Science
edited by
Robert Northcott
Birkbeck, University of London
Jacob Stegenga
University of Cambridge

RELATIVISM IN THE PHILOSOPHY OF SCIENCE

Martin Kusch
University of Vienna

CAMBRIDGE
UNIVERSITY PRESS

CAMBRIDGE
UNIVERSITY PRESS

University Printing House, Cambridge CB2 8BS, United Kingdom

One Liberty Plaza, 20th Floor, New York, NY 10006, USA

477 Williamstown Road, Port Melbourne, VIC 3207, Australia

314–321, 3rd Floor, Plot 3, Splendor Forum, Jasola District Centre, New Delhi – 110025, India

79 Anson Road, #06–04/06, Singapore 079906

Cambridge University Press is part of the University of Cambridge.

It furthers the University's mission by disseminating knowledge in the pursuit of education, learning, and research at the highest international levels of excellence.

www.cambridge.org
Information on this title: www.cambridge.org/9781108969611
DOI: 10.1017/9781108979504

© Martin Kusch 2020

First published 2020

A catalogue record for this publication is available from the British Library.

ISBN 978-1-108-96961-1 Paperback
ISSN 2517-7273 (online)
ISSN 2517-7265 (print)

Relativism in the Philosophy of Science

Elements in the Philosophy of Science

DOI: 10.1017/9781108979504
First published online: December 2020

Martin Kusch
University of Vienna

Author for correspondence: Martin Kusch, martin.kusch@univie.ac.at

Abstract: "Relativism versus absolutism" is one of the fundamental oppositions that have dominated reflections about science for much of its (modern) history. Often these reflections have been inseparable from wider social-political concerns regarding the position of science in society. Where does this debate stand in the philosophy and sociology of science today? And how does the "relativism question" relate to current concerns with "post-truth" politics? In *Relativism in the Philosophy of Science*, Martin Kusch examines some of the most influential relativist proposals of the last fifty years and the controversies they have triggered. He argues that defensible forms of relativism all deny that any sense can be made of a scientific result being absolutely true or justified, and that they all reject "anything goes" – that is, the thought that all scientific results are epistemically on a par. Kusch concludes by distinguishing between defensible forms of relativism and post-truth thinking.

Keywords: relativism, Bas van Fraassen, sociology of knowledge, Barry Barnes, David Bloor, voluntarism

ISBNs: 9781108969611 (PB), 9781108979504 (OC)
ISSNs: 2517-7273 (online), 2517-7265 (print)

Contents

1 Introduction

There are, and have been, many debates around relativism in the philosophy of science. It is impossible to do justice to this volume of work in 30,000 words. I had to choose between a shallow bird's-eye view of the whole terrain and a narrow focus on a small number of positions. In opting for the narrow focus, I was moved by the thought that some other Elements in this series will discuss topics I am setting aside.[1]

Section 2 gives thumbnail sketches both of the spectrum of positions falling under "epistemic relativism" and of influential arguments for and against relativism. Section 3 presents background from the philosophy of science: Thomas Kuhn's work and its reception, Paul Feyerabend's "anarchism," as well as "pluralism" and "perspectivism." Section 4 offers a relativist interpretation of one of the most influential positions in the philosophy of science of recent decades: Bas van Fraassen's "epistemic voluntarism." van Fraassen combines twenty-first-century interests in pluralism and perspectivism with late-twentieth-century preoccupations with Kuhn's and Feyerabend's relativistic ideas. Section 5 presents and defends the relativism of the "Sociology of Scientific Knowledge" (SSK), especially in the version advocated by Barry Barnes and David Bloor. Finally, Section 6 briefly discusses the relationship between relativism and "post-truth" politics.

"Relativism versus absolutism" is one of those fundamental oppositions that have dominated philosophy, religion and science, North and South, East and West, past and present.[2] Despite its omnipresence, the dichotomy "relativism versus absolutism" has not, however, attracted as much historical and philosophical attention as other oppositions. Much work thus remains to be done.

2 What Is Relativism?

This section introduces ways of understanding, motivating, and attacking relativism.

"x Is Relative to y"

One way to categorize different forms of relativism involves the scheme "x is relative to y." Its most important instantiations are the following:[3]

"x" stands for . . .	forms of relativism by subject matter
objects, properties, facts, worlds	. . . ontological

---

[1] See also the relevant papers in Kusch, *Handbook.*   [2] Cf. Kusch, *Handbook.*
[3] Haack, *Manifesto*, p. 149.

truth(s)	... alethic
classifications, concepts, meanings	... semantic
moral values, norms, justifications	... moral
knowledge or epistemic justification	... epistemic
tastes	... gustatory

"y" stands for ...	forms of relativism by context
individuals	... Protagorean
cultures	... cultural
scientific paradigms	... Kuhnian
classes, religions, genders	... standpoint

It is also customary to distinguish between *descriptive, normative,* and *methodological relativisms.* Descriptive relativism makes the empirical claim that there are fundamentally different standards in different contexts. Forms of methodological relativism hold that we should investigate different contexts *as if* they were of equal value. Finally, normative relativism demands that we regard the idea of absolute truths or absolute standards as flawed, absurd, or incoherent.

Ingredients of Epistemic Relativism

Throughout this Element, "relativism" and "absolutism" refer to *epistemic* relativism and *epistemic* absolutism, respectively. Defenders and critics of relativism have put forward various lists of ideas they regard as characteristic of relativism. These tenets should not be understood as necessary and sufficient conditions.[4] Indeed, it is important to keep in mind that none of these elements, on its own, is sufficient as a definition of relativism; it's their various combinations or interpretations that define what one might call "the relativist spectrum."

> (DEPENDENCE) A belief has an epistemic status (e.g. "epistemically justified" or "knowledge") only relative to epistemic standards.

---

[4] Elsewhere I have explained in more detail to whom the different elements might be attributed; see Kusch, "Primer." For different attempts to characterize relativism, see Baghramian and Carter, "Relativism"; Carter, *Metaepistemology*; Baghramian and Coliva, *Relativism*; Seidel, *Epistemic Relativism.*

Different commentators interpret such standards in different ways. "Regularists" think of standards as *rules, principles,* or *norms.*[5] For example, Paul Boghossian claims that we are committed to the following principle:

> (*Observation*) For any observational proposition p, if it visually seems to [subject] X that p and circumstantial conditions D obtain, then X is prima facie justified in believing p.[6]

"Particularists" take our standards to be primarily *particular exemplary epistemic achievements of the past.* For instance, many sixteenth-century astronomers accepted Galileo's telescopic observations of the Moon as work to be emulated.

> (PLURALITY) There is (has been, or could be) more than one set of standards in the same domain; the standards of different sets can conflict. (I shall write "S" for such sets.)

Relativism is thus compatible with the thought that our own S is without an *existing* alternative. It is also worth mentioning that different versions of relativism might have different criteria for deciding how many alternative S there are, or could be.

> (CONFLICT) Epistemic verdicts, based on different S, sometimes exclude one another. This can happen either . . .
> (a) because the two S license incompatible answers to the same question, or
> (b) because the advocates of one S find the answers suggested by the advocates of another S unintelligible.

(a) is an "ordinary" disagreement; (b) captures, as we shall see later, the cases of Kuhnian "incommensurability."[7]

> (CONVERSION) In some cases, switching from one S to another has the character of a "conversion": that is, the switch is underdetermined by S, evidence, or prior beliefs, and is experienced by the converting X as something of a leap of faith.

CONVERSION plays an important role in Kuhn, too. (I shall return to this topic in Section 3.)

> (SYMMETRY) Different S are symmetrical in that they all are:
> (a) based on nothing but local, contingent, and varying causes of credibility (LOCALITY);
> (b) impossible to rank except on the basis of a specific S (NONNEUTRALITY);

---

[5] I take the terminology of "regularism" and "particularism" from Dancy, "Particularism."
[6] Boghossian, *Fear*, p. 84.   [7] Kuhn, *Structure*.

(c) impossible to rank since the evaluative terms of one S are inapplicable to another S (NONAPPRAISABILITY);

(d) equally true or valid (EQUAL VALIDITY).

SYMMETRY is, in many ways, the heart of relativism.[8] It takes different forms, formulated by (a) to (d). LOCALITY runs directly counter to absolutist suggestions according to which there is a unique S that . . .

– ought to be accepted by every rational being;

– enables us to capture truths that "are there anyway"; or

– would be accepted by an ultimate, final science.

LOCALITY allows that the proponents of the standards of one S may (legitimately) criticize the standards of another S. LOCALITY is naturally combined with NONNEUTRALITY: when we rank different S, we must always rely on, or take our starting point from, some other S. A much stronger claim is advanced by NONAPPRAISABILITY.[9] It insists that evaluative terms can only operate *within* an epistemic practice (as defined by a given S). This precludes the option of legitimately evaluating epistemic practices other than one's own. EQUAL VALIDITY goes further still in declaring all S to be equally correct or valid.

Depending on one's selection from, and interpretations of, the five elements, one ends up with different versions of relativism. "Vulgar relativism" results from prioritizing NONAPPRAISABILITY and EQUAL VALIDITY. Most card-carrying relativists therefore reject these elements[10] and thereby allow themselves to criticize other cultures, learn from them, and allow for piecemeal intellectual epistemic change and progress.

Relativist Stances

In the preceding text, relativism was interpreted as a *doctrine* concerning the epistemic status of *beliefs*. Alternatively, we can replace either of the two italicized items with "stances."[11] A stance consists primarily of values, virtues, emotions, policies, and preferences ("VVEPPs") and only secondarily of beliefs. There are three ways to bring the stance-idea to bear on relativism:

---

[8] I take the term "symmetry" from SSK but use it in a wider sense. See Section 5. My LOCALITY aims to capture the position of Barnes and Bloor, "Relativism," 27.

[9] I take this idea from Williams, "Relativism," 132–43.

[10] Barnes and Bloor, "Relativism"; Code, *Rhetorical Spaces*; Field, "Epistemology"; Herrnstein Smith, *Practicing Relativism*; Herbert, *Victorian Relativity*; Feyerabend, *Against Method*.

[11] van Fraassen, *Empirical Stance*.

- relativism may be treated as a *doctrine* about how to conceive of the relation between different epistemic *stances*; VVEPPs then play the role of standards;
- relativism may itself be thought of as a *stance* concerning the relationship between different sets of standards (in the sense of the last section); or
- relativism may be conceived of as a "second-order" stance concerning a set of "first-order" epistemic stances.

What would first-order epistemic stances look like? Consider the conflict between Galileo Galilei and Cardinal Bellarmine.[12] It seems plausible to say that, for Bellarmine, ethical and religious values and virtues interacted closely with epistemic values and made him give special weight to the epistemic virtue of intellectual humility in astronomical and biblical matters. Galileo was also deeply religious, but in studying the natural world he put great emphasis on the epistemic virtues of curiosity, originality, and courage. These differences in virtues and values were entangled with differences in emotions, epistemic policies, and preferences. Of course, Bellarmine and Galileo ultimately also disagreed in their beliefs about the heavens, but perhaps these incompatible beliefs were the result of the exercise of their conflicting virtues and policies.

Why might one conceptualize relativism itself as a stance? It would, for instance, allow one to say that what unites many authors accused of, or happily embracing, forms of relativism is first and foremost a rebellion against absolutist forms of metaphysics, epistemology, or ethics. Many relativists also share further values or virtues: they oppose intellectual imperialism and value epistemic humility or tolerance. Perhaps focusing on these sentiments allows us to identify a tradition of relativist thought that remains invisible for as long as we concentrate on doctrines. Of course, in order for these stances to qualify as relativism, they would have to embody commitments akin to the five elements introduced in the last section.

Why Relativism?

There are more arguments for and against relativism than I can cover here. What follows are no more than quick reminders. I begin with a list of motivations for relativism.

Disagreements – Faultless, Fundamental, Peer

One important way of providing a rationale for relativism centers on disagreements. Some relativists focus on "faultless" disagreements. The paradigmatic examples are gustatory disputes in which two parties differ concerning a "basic

---

[12] Kusch, "Relativist Stances, Virtues and Vices," 282.

taste." In such cases, some relativists insist, both sides may well be *equally right*. If this is correct, then one might go on to ask whether there are other disagreements, in other realms, that trigger the same intuition of faultlessness.[13]

Other relativists look for "fundamental" disagreements in the epistemic realm.[14] Think of two parties differing on whether souls are immortal. The contra-side refers to science; the pro-side draws on the Bible. Assume that both sets of beliefs are consistent and/or in line with their respective standards, and neither side can rationally compel the other to change their beliefs. Some philosophers maintain that relativism is the most charitable response to such a scenario.

Still other relativists draw support from "peer disagreement." Your peers are people who – with respect to a given problem – are as well informed and intelligent as you are yourself. How should you respond when a peer disagrees with you? Suspend judgement? Stick to your own view? Lessen your degree of belief? Count both beliefs relatively justified – in line with relativism? In other words, is it permissible for two peers to arrive at different conclusions even when they have the same evidence? If you opt for "yes," then you are committed to a relativist "permissivism."[15]

Incommensurability

This motivation relates to situations where two parties are unable to fully grasp the meaning of each other's words or thoughts; where – as Kuhn put it – the languages of the two sides are "incommensurable." This limits the reach of argument and threatens the unity of reason. And, if reason is not one but many, relativism looms.[16]

Relativism as a Remedy against Skepticism

A third strategy exploits the fact that absolutism's standards for knowledge or justified belief are hard to meet. This invites skepticism. Shifting from absolutism to relativism lowers the hurdle and thus "saves" our pre-philosophical conviction that we do have many epistemically justified beliefs.[17]

Attacking Absolutist Metaphysics, Semantics, and Philosophy of Science

Relativists have also attacked absolutism by challenging its metaphysical, semantic, or scientific underpinnings. Can we make sense of "truths that are

---

[13] See e.g. Kölbel, "Faultless Disagreement"; MacFarlane, "Relativism"; Wright, "New Age."
[14] Hales, "Motivations."   [15] Hazlett, "Entitlement"; S. Goldberg, pers. conv.
[16] Scheffler, *Science and Subjectivity*.   [17] Sankey, "Witchcraft."

there anyway?" Would creatures shaped by evolution be likely to track absolute truths? Do un-relativized uses of "true" prove that we are implicitly committed to truth-absolutism? Does the notion of an "ultimate science," reaching absolute truth, even make sense?[18] Relativists defend negative answers to all these questions.

Boghossian's Relativist Arguments

Although Paul Boghossian is currently the most influential anti-relativist, he has also suggested prima facie arguments in support of relativism. One argument attacks absolutism head-on. Assume we encounter a group using an S very different from ours. Imagine further that we are not inclined to switch our allegiance from our S to theirs. This inclination needs to be justified based on some S. Which one? Obviously, the only one we have got: ours. But can we really use our S to justify our S? Doesn't this make the justification circular? The relativist urges us to answer "no" to the first question and "yes" to the second. She draws two conclusions. First, we are unable to justify our S. And, second, since every other group of inquirers would find themselves in the same situation, there is no ultimate, absolute justification of any S.[19]

Boghossian's second important relativist argument concerns PLURALITY and consists of offering a historical case of a genuine alternative to our S. The argument presupposes that S consist of more or less fundamental epistemic principles and that we have a genuine alternative to our S if there is a difference *in at least one fundamental principle.* Consider Cardinal Bellarmine.[20] Bellarmine's S included the fundamental epistemic principle "*Revelation*": "For certain propositions p, including propositions about the heavens, believing p is prima facie justified if p is the revealed word of God as claimed by the Bible."[21] Boghossian takes it that many of us today do not accept *Revelation* as an epistemic principle – fundamental or derived. It therefore seems natural to say, given Boghossian's relativist's criteria, that "we" and Bellarmine differ in our epistemic systems: his was a genuine alternative to ours. Furthermore, because of the fundamental position of *Revelation* in Bellarmine's S, we cannot easily – if at all – convince him to drop *Revelation*. We cannot show him that *Revelation* fails to follow from principles that we share with him. Boghossian's relativist concludes that Bellarmine's S is as valid as our own.[22]

---

[18] Bloor, "Epistemic Grace"; Bloor, "Relativism"; Field, "Epistemology"; Street, "Evolution."
[19] Boghossian, *Fear*, pp. 76–7.   [20] Feyerabend, *Against Method*; Rorty, *Philosophy.*
[21] Boghossian, *Fear*, p. 69.   [22] Ibid.

Some Arguments against Relativism

I do not have the space here to introduce rejoinders to all the relativist arguments sketched earlier. Given their influence, it seems appropriate to give prominence to Boghossian's criticisms.

Boghossian versus Boghossian

Boghossian has two objections to the circularity argument. First, there is no onus on us to defend sticking to our S when we encounter an alternative. We must do so only when the alternative is "impressive enough to make us legitimately doubt the correctness of our own epistemic system."[23] After all, if there is nothing impressive about the alternative, why take it seriously? Why see it as a potential threat to our own S? Second, using S to justify S is allowed as long as S has not become independently doubtful.[24]

As far as Bellarmine is concerned, Boghossian denies that Bellarmine's S is a genuine alternative to ours. If *Revelation* was fundamental for Bellarmine, his use of it should be dismissed as "arbitrary": Bellarmine used *Revelation* to dismiss heliocentrism but ignored *Revelation* when inquiring about other celestial matters, like whether the sun was shining.[25] Boghossian's "charitable" alternative is to say that *Revelation* was *not fundamental* for Bellarmine and that he had reasons for the selective application of *Revelation*. But then we no longer have a genuine alternative to our S.

Self-Refutation

Boghossian formulates this classic attack on relativism as follows:

> The claim "Nothing is objectively justified, but only justified relative to this or that epistemic system" must be nonsense, for it would itself have to be either objectively justified, or only justified relative to this or that particular epistemic system. But it can't be objectively justified, since in that case it would be false if true. And it can't be justified only relative to the relativist's epistemic system, since in that case it is just a report of what he finds it agreeable to say. If he also invites us to join him, we need not offer any reason for declining since he has offered us no reason to accept.[26]

Boghossian finds the argument unconvincing. It rests on the questionable assumption that the relativist stands *outside our* community. If the relativist is a member of our culture, the relativist and the rest of us share the same S. And then the relativist might insist that his position is "justified by principles that are endorsed by relativists and non-relativists alike."[27]

---

[23] Ibid., p. 101.   [24] Ibid., p. 100.   [25] Ibid., p. 104.   [26] Ibid., p. 83.
[27] Ibid.; cf. Boghossian, "Epistemic Reasons," 27.

Still, Boghossian believes that the self-refutation charge can be reformulated. He takes it to be central to relativism that one's choice of standards is ultimately unconstrained by higher or absolute standards. We therefore are "epistemically blameless" if we so choose our epistemic standards that whatever we want to believe ends up being justified. If that is correct, however, the absolutist opponent of relativism is entitled to so pick her epistemic standards that relativism turns out to be unjustified. Relativism refutes itself.[28]

Relativist Double-Think

Boghossian also highlights a difficulty with respect to how relativists think about their anti-relativist opponents. Assume I am a relativist and encounter Otto, who, based on his reading of fairy tales, believes in ghosts. I reject Otto's belief based on scientific knowledge. As a relativist, I believe that our respective judgements are both epistemically justified relative to our respective S and that thus both of our judgements are "faultless."

And yet, if I judge validly that . . .

(a) *Belief in ghosts is not justified*
    . . . then it is also right for me to think that . . .
(b) *It's true that belief in ghosts is not justified.*
    Moreover, if I accept (b) then I also have to commit to . . .
(c) *It's false that belief in ghosts is justified.*
    And in light of (c) I have to conclude that . . .
(d) *Anyone who judges that belief in ghosts is justified is making a mistake.*

But (d) contradicts the relativist view that the disagreement is faultless.[29]

One possible reply involves two perspectives: the perspective of the committed knower and the perspective of the relativist theoretician.[30] When I take my disagreement with Otto to be faultless, I adopt the latter perspective. When I believe that Otto has made a mistake, I speak from the perspective of the committed knower. Since the perspectives are separate, there is no direct conflict between the two judgements. Boghossian is not convinced. If I occupy both perspectives, he says, then I suffer from "serious cognitive dissonance": I take Otto's judgement to be both faultless and faulty at the same time.[31]

---

[28] Boghossian, "Epistemic Reasons," 30–1.   [29] Boghossian, "Three Kinds," 62.
[30] Boghossian, "Relativismus," 386–7.   [31] Ibid.

Against Absolute Relativism

Some forms of relativism work with a mixture of absolute and relative principles. Think of a relativism of manners based on the one absolute principle: "When in Rome do as the Romans do" or of subjective Bayesians for whom the Bayesian formula is the one and only absolute principle.[32] Boghossian rejects such "absolute relativism" for two reasons. First, one of the best arguments against absolutism asks how absolute principles could possibly fit into a contingent empirical world. In allowing at least one such principle, absolute relativism has foregone the right to use this argument. Boghossian's second reason for dismissing absolute relativism is that it has no good answer to this question: if there can be at least one absolute principle, why can't there be many?[33]

Variation

Boghossian readily acknowledges that our epistemic practices vary, but he denies that such variation supports relativism. What variation there is can be explained by the fact that our absolute rules are sometimes vague and unspecific. They leave room for choice.[34]

3 Kuhn, Feyerabend, Perspectivism, Pluralism

Introduction

In this section I continue preparing the ground with brief reminders concerning recent Kuhn-debates, Feyerabend, pluralism, and perspectivism.

Kuhn's Structure

The Structure of Scientific Revolutions proposes a cyclical model of the development of "mature" natural sciences. From time to time, "normal science" falls into "crises"; these crises lead to "revolutions," which in turn result in new forms of normal science. Normal science is based on "paradigms." On the one hand, paradigms are "exemplars," that is, outstanding scientific achievements that scientists seek to emulate and that are central in training and textbooks. On the other hand, "paradigms" are "disciplinary matrices" consisting of shared equations, metaphysical commitments, cognitive values, and exemplars. Exemplars are primary with respect to rules and standards. Normal science is comparable to "puzzle-solving."

---

[32] Boghossian, "Three Kinds," 67.　　[33] Ibid., p. 68.
[34] Boghossian, pers. comm.; cf. Boghossian, *Fear*, p. 110.

Normal science invariably encounters problems that cannot be successfully tackled using the ruling paradigm. When such "anomalies" start piling up, the respective scientific field enters a period of crisis. For the scientists involved, the world seems "out of joint." Scientists begin debating the foundations of their field. The eventual emergence of a new paradigm is analogous to a political revolution. The choice between the old and the new paradigm(s) is a choice between incompatible forms of life. The main reason for the incompatibility is "incommensurability": the new paradigm radically changes the meaning of central scientific terms or comes with fundamentally new values and methodologies. Accepting the new paradigm is not rationally mandated by the standards of the old paradigm. The switch is therefore akin to a "conversion" and a "Gestalt-shift." After the switch, scientists live in a "new world." Kuhn finds it implausible to describe this development as a progress towards the truth. He prefers to capture the dynamics in evolutionary terms; scientific disciplines improve their adaptation by solving problems.

Kuhn after *Structure*

In his later writings, Kuhn focuses increasingly on "taxonomies" and holds that scientific revolutions involve substantive changes in such "lexica." Incompatible taxonomies make word-for-word translation across paradigms impossible.[35] But Kuhn now rejects his earlier talk of Gestalt-shifts. As concerns theory choice, he stresses the role of epistemic values like accuracy, consistency, scope, simplicity. and fruitfulness. Still, Kuhn insists that different scientists may rationally favor some values over others; interpret a given value differently; or resolve conflicts between these values in variant ways.[36]

The later Kuhn gives considerable attention to the formation of new scientific specialties. Indeed, processes of discipline-splitting are now identified as an alternative to the across-the-board replacement of an old paradigm by a new one. Fields resulting from such splits use incommensurable lexica or taxonomies.

Finally, in his later work, Kuhn increasingly favors a Kantian rendering of his position,[37] writing, for instance: "Like the Kantian categories, the lexicon supplies preconditions of possible experience. But lexical categories, unlike their Kantian forebears, can and do change, both with time and with the passage from one community to another."[38]

---

[35] Kuhn, *Road since Structure*, p. 93.   [36] Kuhn, *Essential Tension*, pp. 320–39.
[37] From Hoyningen-Huene, *Reconstructing*.   [38] Kuhn, *Road since Structure*, p. 104.

Recent Kuhn-Debates

Kuhn's cyclical "structure" for the development of natural-scientific disciplines is today often rejected. As Lorraine Daston reports, "[m]ost historians of science no longer believe that any kind of structure could possibly do justice to their subject matter."[39] Daniel Garber complains that the Scientific Revolution did not result in the adoption of *one* new paradigm but in a "diversity of competing alternatives."[40] Card-carrying pluralists like Peter Galison and Hasok Chang[41] agree. Galison approvingly quotes Feyerabend's objection to Kuhn: "Your hidden predilection for monism (for one paradigm) leads you to a false report of historical events."[42] Other critics object that Kuhn's "structure" does not fit the quantum revolution,[43] interdisciplinary research,[44] recent physics or biology,[45] or the Darwinian revolution.[46] Still, some commentators find Kuhn helpful for understanding the Chemical Revolution[47] or seek to build on Kuhn's insights by offering more fine-grained taxonomies for scientific revolutions.[48]

Present-day philosophers of science also disagree over incommensurability. For Howard Sankey, incommensurability "is no longer a live issue": all that remains – after Kuhn's own revisions – is the trivial idea that sometimes understanding a scientific theory demands great effort.[49] Ronald Giere reaches a similar conclusion.[50] Some authors who focus specifically on Kuhn's taxonomic rendering of incommensurability have been equally dismissive.[51] Other philosophers see things more positively. Chang finds Kuhn's ideas on methodological and value incommensurability important,[52] and Alexander Bird wants to "naturalize" incommensurability by making it depend upon differences in mental schemata, analogical thinking, or pattern recognition.[53]

The very different perspectives on Kuhn also incorporate conflicting views on the value of exemplars. Daston speaks of "the now-vulgar 'paradigm'" and laments that no-one to date has "succeeded in hammering out a systematic, analytic language for talking about knowledge without rules."[54] Angela Creager demurs, claiming that model organisms and systems "function quite

[39] Daston, "History of Science," 117.   [40] Garber, "Scientific Revolution," 143.
[41] Chang, *Water.*   [42] Galison, "Practice," 64.   [43] Timmins, "History and Philosophy."
[44] Mizrahi, "Kuhn's Incommensurability"; Argamakova, "Modeling."
[45] Galison, "Practice"; Hacking, "Essay."
[46] Mayr, "Darwinian Revolution"; Greene, "Kuhnian Paradigm"; Argamakova, "Modeling."
[47] Chang, *Water*; Hoyningen-Huene, "Thomas Kuhn."
[48] McMullin, "Rationality"; Wray, *Kuhn's Epistemology*, pp. 12–22; cf. Andersen, Barker, and Chen, *Cognitive Structure.*
[49] Sankey, "Demise," 87.   [50] Giere, *Perspectivism*, loc. 1166–9.
[51] Mizrahi, "Kuhn's Incommensurability." Cf. Patton, "Kuhn, Pedagogy."   [52] Chang, *Water.*
[53] Bird, "Incommensurability."   [54] Daston, "History of Science," 117, 125.

clearly as exemplars in Kuhn's sense."[55] But Creager's paradigms are not as stable as Kuhn's: they are "changeable points of reference amidst the day-to-day decisions that are constitutive of research."[56]

Paul Teller emphasizes that contemporary concerns with models are naturally related to Kuhn's exemplars. Scientific training consists of developing the skills needed for "applying one or another model building tool kit."[57] A scientific theory is primarily a "range of models"; these can be shared between disciplines and migrate from one discipline to another. This makes the boundaries of scientific theories vague.[58] Teller believes that his reconceptualizing of exemplars as models supports Kuhn's skepticism about "absolute, context-independent, trans-paradigmatic comparisons of closeness to the truth." Talk of closeness to the truth makes sense only "in a contextualized, interest-relative way." "Closeness to the truth" is but a special case of "similarity," and "there is no absolute notion of similarity."[59] We assess models with respect to how well they "contribute to and detract from a wide range of our practical and cognitive epistemic ends." There is no "common measure" for them all.[60]

As we shall see later, the emphasis on models is also central for van Fraassen. Bird[61] notes another parallel between Kuhn and van Fraassen: the emphasis upon empirical adequacy as the goal of natural science and thus a studied refusal to commit to the theoretical entities postulated by our theories. Kuhn writes that "[t]he scientist can have no recourse above and beyond what he sees with his eyes and instruments."[62] And for Kuhn the ultimate aim of the puzzle-solving of science is an ever-closer fit between "theory and the results of experiment and observation."[63]

Finally, the question whether Kuhn is an "externalist" and "relativist" has remained central. Philosophical commentators agree that Kuhn is an "internalist" insofar as he seeks to explain theory change by focusing on anomalies and debates *within* scientific disciplines.[64] Bird insists that the difference between Kuhn and "externalist" sociologists lies in their respective conception of rationality: allegedly the sociologists have a "thin" conception that, even combined with empirical data, is unable to determine theory choice. To close the gap, the sociologists therefore need to bring in social-political interests. Kuhn does not need to do so, since he has a "thick" conception of rationality which includes epistemic values and skills.[65]

According to Michael Friedman,[66] Kuhn's conception of scientific revolutions is relativistic. Friedman seeks to defend "universal (trans-historical)

[55] Creager, "Paradigms," 152.   [56] Ibid., 154.   [57] Teller, "Idealizations," 248.
[58] Lange, *Introduction*, p. 283.   [59] Teller, "Idealizations," 255–6.   [60] Ibid., 263.
[61] Bird, *Kuhn*, p. 145.   [62] Kuhn, *Structure*, loc. 2316.   [63] Bird, *Kuhn*, p. 145.
[64] Bird, "Kuhn, Naturalism."   [65] Ibid., 216–21.
[66] Friedman, *Dynamics*; Friedman, "Extending the Dynamics."

scientific rationality" against Kuhn.[67] Friedman rejects Kuhn's value-based account of paradigm choice as a case of mere "subjective" "instrumental rationality." Instead, what matters in science is "objective ... communicative rationality," the rationality involved in finding a rational consensus on questions of truth and falsity.[68] Moreover, scientific revolutions are *prospectively* as well as *retrospectively* fully rational: prospectively, since the path from the old to the new paradigm consists of rational and intelligible small steps; retrospectively, since laws and principles of the old paradigm are preserved as approximate special cases in the new paradigm. Philosophy is an actor in scientific revolutions, since it procures "inter-paradigm rationality."[69] But philosophers are also analysts: by showing that and how all phases of science are rational, philosophers "take reflective responsibility" for science in general. For instance, philosophy shows that current science is "an approximation to a final, ideal community of inquiry ... that has achieved a universal, transhistorical communicative rationality on the basis of the fully general and adequate constitutive principles reached in the ideal limit of scientific progress."[70]

Feyerabend

Although the slogan "anything goes" still plays a significant role in relativism-debates – roughly, as shorthand for EQUAL VALIDITY[71] – Feyerabend's wider philosophical concerns are no longer discussed in mainstream philosophy, history, and sociology of science. Still, a few reminders of some central relativistic themes in *Against Method* will prove useful later. (Limitations of space prevent me from discussing the secondary literature.)

The core of *Against Method* is "epistemic anarchism." It can be summed up as a protest against all "attempts to regiment scientific" work by alleged "universal standards, universal laws, [or] universal ideas like 'Truth', 'Reason', 'Justice', 'Love'."[72] More generally, the "idea of a ... fixed theory of rationality rests on too naïve a view of man and his social surroundings."[73] Accordingly, the anarchist has "no everlasting loyalty to, and no everlasting aversion against, any institution or any ideology."[74] Anarchists are therefore committed "pluralists" fighting for the coexistence of conflicting scientific theories.[75]

The central case study of *Against Method* is Galileo's fight for heliocentrism. One important theme is that epistemology was (and is) no neutral arbiter in fundamental scientific disagreements:

---

[67] Friedman, *Dynamics*, loc. 2547.   [68] Ibid., loc. 1195.   [69] Ibid., loc. 1424.
[70] Ibid., loc. 1391–5.   [71] Boghossian, "Epistemic Reasons."
[72] Feyerabend, *Against Method*, pp. 19 and 189.   [73] Ibid., p. 27.   [74] Ibid., p. 189.
[75] Ibid., pp. 43, 53.

Astronomy, physics, psychology, *epistemology* – all these disciplines collaborate in the Aristotelian philosophy to create a system that is coherent, rational and in agreement with the results of observation as can be seen from an examination of Aristotelian philosophy in the form in which it was developed by some mediaeval philosophers.[76]

Particularly influential within Aristotelian epistemology was a "naïve realism with respect to motion," according to which "apparent motion is identical with real (absolute) motion."[77] In order to challenge this naïve realism, Galileo had to introduce a "new kind of experience." He had to persuade his audience that the motion of the Earth was real even though it could not be observed. In so doing, Galileo introduced a new epistemology.[78] Lacking a neutral intellectual arbiter, Galileo used "propaganda," "psychological tricks," "clever techniques of persuasion," "emotion," and "appeal to prejudices of all kinds."[79] Scientific revolutionaries succeed because "they do not permit themselves to be bound by 'laws of reason', 'standards of rationality', or 'immutable laws of nature'."[80] Moreover, the victory of Copernicanism depended upon the emergence of the rise of "a new secular class" for which the new astronomy represented "progress," "the classical times of Plato and Cicero," and "a free and pluralistic society."[81]

In light of this, it is perhaps surprising that Feyerabend insists that "Ptolemy and Copernicus" were not strictly incommensurable.[82] *Against Method* holds that two theories are commensurable or incommensurable *only under an interpretation*. For instance, Feyerabend writes that "instrumentalism ... makes commensurable all those theories which are related to the same observation language and are interpreted on its basis."[83] Thus, Ptolemy and Copernicus may well be incommensurable under the interpretations of seventeenth-century Aristotelians or Galileo but well-nigh commensurable under the interpretation of, say, Tycho Brahe.

Still, *Against Method* describes the interval between the reigns of geo- and heliocentrism as a time in which increasing numbers of natural philosophers were willing to support a view that they recognized as "inconsistent with [...] plain and obvious [facts]" and with well-established theories.[84] It took "sheer pig-headedness"[85] to come up with a new theory: "the 'irrationality' of the transition period [is] overcome [...] by the determined production of nonsense until the material produced is rich enough to permit the rebels to reveal, and everyone else to recognize, new universal principles."[86]

---

[76] Ibid., p. 149; emphasis added.   [77] Ibid., pp. 75, 90.   [78] Ibid., p. 153.
[79] Ibid., pp. 89, 81, 106, 143, 154.   [80] Ibid., p. 191.   [81] Ibid. p. 154.
[82] Ibid., pp. 23, 95, 114, 305.   [83] Ibid., p. 279.   [84] Ibid., p. 56.   [85] Ibid., p. 155.
[86] Ibid., p. 270.

Scientific Pluralism

Over the last two decades, Feyerabend's previously cited call for "pluralism" has found increasing support.[87] I shall focus on Chang's book *Is Water H₂O?* Chang calls his position "active normative epistemic pluralism" and characterizes it as "the doctrine advocating the cultivation of multiple systems of practice in any given field of science"[88]: "Each system of practice is conducive to revealing particular aspects of reality, and by cultivating multiple incommensurable systems we stand to gain most knowledge."[89]

Chang offers various general motivations for pluralism. Most important is the appeal to humility and prudence: since the world is inexhaustibly complex, we are better off with multiple approaches.[90] The benefits of pluralism are said to be of two kinds: there are "benefits of toleration" and "benefits of interaction."[91] The former are "hedging our bets" (it is prudent to have multiple lines of inquiry); "division of domain" (it is wise to use different theoretical tools in the same domain); "satisfaction of different aims" (no one scientific system can satisfy all needs and values); and "multiple satisfaction" ("epistemic abundance should delight us"). Benefits of interaction are "integration," "co-optation" (think of competitors using each other's results), and "competition."

Chang aims to justify his *normative* pluralism also on the basis of *descriptive* pluralism. He puts forward a novel interpretation of the Chemical Revolution. For instance, he tries to show that Lavoisier's position was opposed much longer than is usually assumed[92] and that the Chemical Revolution ultimately was due to a long-term trend called "compositionism." Compositionists divide substances into "elements" and "compounds." All elements are equally fundamental and compounds are determinable through the use of the balance. The alternative to compositionism is "principlism," a dualistic conception involving imponderable fundamental principles and passive substances.[93] The oxygenist view fitted better into the compositionist trend than the phlogistonist system. The relevance of this thesis for pluralism seems to be that compositionism and principlism are too basic for us to be able to choose between them. Both should be kept alive. Turning from questions of explanation to comparison and evaluation, Chang wishes to establish a *symmetry* between the phlogiston and the oxygen theories: both are "equally wrong, from the modern point of view" and both were "partially successful."[94] There thus was "no reason to clearly favor one over the other."[95] Both should have been pursued.

---

[87] Dupre, *Disorder of Things*; Kellert, Longino, and Waters (eds.), *Pluralism*; Chang, *Water*.
[88] Chang, *Water*, pp. 260, 268.   [89] Ibid., p. 218.   [90] Ibid., p. 255.   [91] Ibid., pp. 279–84.
[92] Ibid., p. 29.   [93] Ibid., p. 40.   [94] Ibid., p. 10.   [95] Ibid., p. 29.

Scientific Perspectivism

Although its origins are sometimes traced back to Kant and Nietzsche,[96] scientific perspectivism has gained prominence only recently, primarily due to the work of Giere and Michela Massimi.[97] Massimi characterizes perspectivism broadly as the claim that scientific knowledge is "historically ... and/or ... culturally situated."[98]

Giere's *Scientific Perspectivism* makes a case for perspectivism on three levels: color perception, scientific instrumental observation, and theories. As far as color perception is concerned, Giere starts from the difference between "dichromats" (who mix two wavelengths of light) and "trichromats" (who mix three): dichromats and trichromats have different "color perspectives." Propositions about the sameness or differences of colors are relative to these perspectives. And it makes no sense to say that these perspectives themselves are either true or false. Still, trichromats are able to draw more color-related distinctions than dichromats. For Giere, his position is a form of "perspectival realism": "perspectival" because claims about the colors of objects are meaningless unless we specify color perspectives. And yet, "color perspectives are intersubjectively objective" in that "most people generally see the same objects as similarly colored in similar circumstances."[99] And in color perception "we perceive aspects of the world itself."[100]

Giere's account of scientific instrumental observation is perspectival-realist in pretty much the same way. For instance, the "Advanced Camera for Surveys" aboard the "Hubble Telescope" collects astronomical data in the near-infrared regions of the electromagnetic spectrum; the "Compton Gamma Ray Observatory" collects astronomical data by detecting gamma rays.[101] The two instruments provide us with different perspectives on the universe. And "claims about what is observed cannot be detached from the means of observation"[102]: "to be an object detected in several different perspectives is not to be detected in no perspective whatsoever."[103] At the same time, instruments "respond to ... aspects of their environment."[104]

Finally, scientific theorizing is also perspectival. This is especially clear when Giere compares scientific models to maps. Think of the "Mercator-" and "Peters-projections." The two projections give us "incompatible" perspectives on the surface of the Earth. This shows that scientists' "methodological

---

[96] Massimi, "Perspectivism," 165.
[97] Massimi, "Perspectivism"; Giere, *Perspectivism*; cf. Massimi and McCoy (eds.), *Understanding Perspectivism*.
[98] Massimi, "Perspectivism," 164.   [99] Giere, *Perspectivism*, loc. 224.
[100] Ibid., loc. 511–14.   [101] Ibid., loc. 621, 651.   [102] Ibid., loc. 684–5.
[103] Ibid., loc. 805–6.   [104] Ibid., loc. 591–2.

presumption ... that different perspectives on a single universe should, in principle, be compatible" may not be right.[105] Just like maps, so also scientific theories (qua collections of models) are "perspectives within which to conceive of aspects of the world."[106] If these models have been empirically confirmed, then scientists are realists about these aspects. This realism remains perspectival,[107] but it rejects agnosticism about theoretical entities as "quixotic," as totally out of touch with how scientists reason themselves.[108]

Relativism?

Kuhn's and Feyerabend's theorizing, pluralism, perspectivism – how do these positions relate to the taxonomy of relativist positions outlined in Section 2?[109]

Kuhn, Feyerabend, Chang, and Giere clearly accept DEPENDENCE. For Kuhn and Feyerabend, scientific judgements, beliefs, and actions are relative to paradigms, taxonomies, or standards; for Chang they are relative to systems of practice; and for Giere they are relative to perspectives. As far as the distinction between "regularists" and "particularists" is concerned, only Kuhn is firmly particularist.

All four positions accept PLURALITY, though with different emphasis. At least the 1962-Kuhn is strongly *monist* about mature natural science. Accordingly, the plurality of paradigms is more diachronic than synchronic. Still, Kuhn deems diachronic PLURALITY essential for the progress of science. The later Kuhn is interested in discipline-splitting; this move introduces PLURALITY also as an important *synchronic* feature. The later Kuhn is thus no longer straightforwardly monist. Feyerabend argues for synchronic as well as diachronic pluralism from the start. Giere also accepts a PLURALITY of perspectives, at least as a possibility. Chang is committed to PLURALITY not only as a *descriptive* thesis, but also as a *normative* program. It is debatable whether this is a step *beyond* relativism.

CONFLICT allowed for two options: that the advocates of paradigm P_1 find the answers given by advocates of another paradigm P_2 *incompatible* with their own answers, or that they find the answers based on P_2 *unintelligible* (in the light of P_1). The latter option was meant to be tailor-made for strong forms of incommensurability. There can be little doubt that Kuhn accepts at least the "incompatibility" version of CONFLICT. The same is true of Feyerabend. Both Kuhn and Feyerabend are also ready to defend CONVERSION: after all, the switch to a new paradigm typically is not uniquely prescribed or licensed by the old paradigm's standards in combination with strong evidence. As we saw

---

[105] Ibid., loc. 1124–5.   [106] Ibid., loc. 824.   [107] Ibid., loc. 1129–30.   [108] Ibid., loc. 1234.
[109] Here I am indebted to Veigl, "Testing Scientific Pluralism."

earlier, Giere rejects talk of semantic incommensurability. And yet, as his discussion of the Mercator- and Peters-projections makes clear enough, he recognizes incompatibilities amongst perspectives. Chang's position is more flexible than Giere's: although compositionism and principlism have the ring of incommensurable viewpoints, Chang deems it an open question – to be decided by historical work – whether and to what extent semantic and methodological incommensurability play a role. Perhaps the same should be said about Chang's position vis-à-vis CONVERSION.

Finally, as far as SYMMETRY is concerned, there is no indication that any of our three authors supports EQUAL VALIDITY. It seems that when Feyerabend rejects "skepticism,"[110] Kuhn "mere relativism,"[111] Chang "just relativism,"[112] or Giere "silly relativism,"[113] they have EQUAL VALIDITY in mind. Of course, this leaves us with the question of what nonskeptical anarchism or "nonmere," "nonjust," or "nonsilly" relativism amounts to. And it seems natural to say that for the four philosophers it amounts to a relativism defined in terms of at least NONNEUTRALITY and perhaps also LOCALITY.

To conclude, all four positions fall within the spectrum of relativism outlined in Section 2.

4 Epistemic Voluntarism and Relativism

Introduction

In this section I shall interpret Bas van Fraassen's philosophy of science as a sophisticated form of relativism. Admittedly, van Fraassen has distanced himself from "debilitating relativism."[114] But this leaves, of course, "nondebilitating" relativism in the running.[115]

In the first subsection, I shall highlight relativistic motifs in *The Scientific Image* (= "*Image*")[116] and *Scientific Representation* (= "*Representation*").[117] Subsequently, I shall outline the relativist position in *The Empirical Stance* (= "*Stance*").[118] In the final subsection, I shall critically discuss van Fraassen's position.

---

[110] Feyerabend, *Against Method*, p. 189.   [111] Kuhn, *Structure*, loc. 3695.

[112] Chang, *Water*, p. 261.   [113] Giere, *Perspectivism*, loc. 215.

[114] van Fraassen, "Reply to Chakravartty."

[115] I am not, of course, the first reader to classify van Fraassen's views as relativist. Cf. Chakravartty, "Stance Relativism"; Ladyman, "Scientistic Stance"; Chakravartty, *Scientific Ontology*.

[116] van Fraassen, *Scientific Image*.   [117] van Fraassen, *Representation*.

[118] van Fraassen, *Empirical Stance*.

Relativism-Related Motifs in *The Scientific Image* and *Scientific Representation*

Image and *Representation* contain many motifs that fit with the relativism in *Stance*. There are six such motifs in *Image*.

The first is "anti-realism" about theoretical entities. The core idea is the claim that science "aims to give us theories which are empirically adequate; and acceptance of a theory involves as belief only that it is empirically adequate. ... [a] theory is empirically adequate exactly if what it says about the observable things and events in this world is true."[119] This empiricist anti-realism – although not relativist by itself – creates a space for relativist views, at least once it is combined with the further assumption that more than one theory can be empirically adequate.

The second relevant theme in *Image* is the thought that "scientific activity is one of construction rather than discovery: [the] construction of models."[120] This "constructionism" is part and parcel of the "semantic approach to theories," that is, the thought that to present a theory is first and foremost to identify "its models."[121] And a theory is "empirically adequate" to the extent that certain parts of its models have "empirical substructures" that directly represent observable phenomena.[122] van Fraassen's emphasis on construction *rather than discovery* gives relativism an important argumentative tool by highlighting the – potentially very different – human contributions to the shaping of scientific knowledge.

The third relativism-related *topos* in *Image* is "the hermeneutic circle." van Fraassen uses this term to express a mutual dependence between two or more elements. The idea is pertinent for understanding observability. There is a hermeneutic circle concerning observability *within the sciences* insofar as they use observation in order to identify the limits of observation. There is a further hermeneutic circle in the relationship *between the empirical sciences and philosophy*: philosophy tells us how the empirical sciences depend upon observations, and, in doing so, philosophy draws on the empirical sciences' findings concerning observation and its limits.[123] There is no absolute *punctum archimedis* concerning observability in either science or philosophy.

The fourth idea, "anthropocentrism," surfaces in the notion of the observing human body as a measuring instrument:

> observation is a special subspecies of measurement.[124] [And the] human
> organism is, from the point of view of physics, a certain kind of measuring

---

[119] van Fraassen, *Scientific Image*, loc. 10,923.   [120] Ibid., loc. 7,867–8.
[121] Ibid., loc. 24,905.   [122] Ibid., loc. 33,644.   [123] Ibid., loc. 30,587.
[124] Ibid., loc. 31,459.

apparatus. As such it has certain inherent limitations . . . It is these limitations to which the "able" in "observable" refers.[125]

Since empirical science is based upon what is observable *for humans*, it invariably is "anthropocentric."[126] Science cannot transcend the human perspective, and we cannot arrive at a "view from nowhere." Early-twentieth-century absolutists like Edmund Husserl called this type of relativism "anthropologism."[127]

Fifth, *Image* also harbors a *historicist-relativist-Kantian* thought. It relates to the thesis that to accept a theory involves "immersion in [its] theoretical world-picture."[128] This "conceptual framework through which I perceive and conceive the world" has as its "intentional correlate" the "world in which I live, breathe and have my being, and which my ancestors of two centuries ago could not enter."[129] This is reminiscent of Kuhn's famous relativistic claim that advocates of different paradigms live literally in different worlds. To be sure, van Fraassen adds that "the real world" is always "the same" and that "conceptual relativism" is to be rejected.[130] Maybe so, but he seems to reject conceptual relativism only concerning the "noumenal world," not concerning "phenomenal worlds." This does not mean that van Fraassen rejects progress; he is adamant that we have "many experimental findings" that "cannot be accommodated in the science of an earlier time." But he immediately adds that this is progress in terms of empirical adequacy and not in terms of truth.[131]

Sixth, and finally, it fits with van Fraassen's other relativism-related motifs that he also opposes treating "objectivity" as a neutral measuring stick for worldviews. Objectivity versus subjectivity is "an intra-scientific distinction": their criteria change from worldview to worldview. For instance, electrons are objective or real, and "flying horses" subjective or fictitious, only for someone "immersed" in the "world-view" of modern science.[132]

Representation is van Fraassen's *chef d'oeuvre*. In our context it is imperative to highlight that *Representation* provides a unifying framework for a variety of relativistic motifs. The central concept is the "Wittgensteinian" idea of "indexicality": the notion that all aspects of scientific representation have to be analyzed in terms of varying goals, individual and collective agency, interests, conceptual resources, and interpretations.

This perspective is very much in evidence in *Representation*'s discussion of measurement. Measuring presupposes a "coordination" between states of the measuring device and states of the measured objects. Establishing such coordination is possible only with the help of further measuring devices, theories,

---

[125] Ibid., loc. 13,110–11. [126] Ibid., loc. 31,459. [127] Husserl, *Logical Investigations*.
[128] van Fraassen, *Scientific Image*, loc. 41,072. [129] Ibid., loc. 41,972.
[130] Ibid., loc. 41,072. [131] Ibid., loc. 41,509. [132] Ibid., loc. 41,507.

and, ultimately, the human body. These are the anthropocentric and historicist dimensions familiar from *Image*. *Representation* adds that measurements are "representations ... made with a purpose or goal in mind, governed by criteria of adequacy pertaining to that goal, which guide its means, medium, and selectivity."[133] Every representation involves some "distortion, infidelity, lack of resemblance in some respects"[134] as well as "surplus structure."[135] van Fraassen insists that these features can only be adequately captured if we "understand them in terms of pragmatics, referring to contexts of use."[136] No process is a measurement unless a given group of scientists, in light of specific theoretical assumptions, goals, and interests, *takes it to be* a measurement. Moreover, measurement does not end with reading instruments. Measurement includes the construction of representational "data models" and (mathematical) "surface models."

The anti-realist and relativist upshot of this "indexicalism" becomes clear in van Fraassen's attack on "structural realism." Structural realism combines two theses: that, historically, equations rather than entities accumulate and get subsumed under successor theories; and that it is correspondence between equations and structures of the natural world that best explains the predictive success of our theories. van Fraassen's critique is centered on the idea that mathematical structure on its own is not natural science. For us *to use* the mathematical structure for purposes of explanation or understanding, we need to locate ourselves relative to it – as we need to locate ourselves on a map in order to find our way. We need to match elements of the mathematics with elements in the world. The mathematical structure itself does not do this for us. van Fraassen calls this idea "Wittgensteinian, in that it focuses on us, on our use of theories and representations ... A theory says nothing to us unless we locate ourselves, in our own language, with respect to its content."[137] It follows that the predictive success of our scientific theories cannot be attributed to mathematical equations alone. Structural realism thus does not stand in the way of empiricist anti-realism.

van Fraassen also turns against Giere's perspectival realism. The different uses of the map-metaphor are telling. For Giere, the central issue concerning maps is *semantic*: what information is encoded in the map? On which features of the world does the map open a perspectival window? For van Fraassen the central issue is *pragmatic*, something that is incorrectly frozen and reified in the process of "abstract[ing] obliviously from use to use-independent concepts."[138] From the perspective of pragmatics, we ask "how is a given subject situating herself relative to the map and the terrain?," "how is she matching features of

---

[133] van Fraassen, *Representation*, loc. 228.   [134] Ibid., loc. 301.   [135] Ibid., loc. 648.
[136] Ibid., loc. 480.   [137] Ibid., loc. 4,326–8.   [138] Ibid., loc. 4,326.

the map to features of the world?," and "how and why, and in light of what goals and aims does she take the map to be accurate?" Moreover, for van Fraassen, Giere's perspectival realism (especially concerning instruments) is based on a problematic metaphor of instruments as "windows into the invisible world."[139] As *Representation* has it, so far from constituting an argument for scientific realism, the window-metaphor actually presupposes realism from the start. *Representation* suggests an alternative that is less committal: that scientific instruments and experiments are "engines" that "create new observable phenomena."[140] The talk of "creation" here parallels earlier descriptions in *Image* of scientific work as construction rather than discovery.

We can also highlight the crucial difference between Giere and van Fraassen in terms of their guiding "exemplars." For Giere the central exemplar for perspectivism is the operation of our trichromat *physiology*. It fixes what colors we can see. There is no choice, no agency, no intentional interpretation, no relevant indexicality. When Giere renders instruments and theories in parallel fashion, they become equally impersonal, inflexible, and the same for all users. For van Fraassen the central exemplar is the artist, the painter or sculptor, or the interpreter of a work of art. This highlights intentional creation and construction in light of variable goals and aims in particular circumstances. Put differently, van Fraassen is not so much focused on what perspectives force us to see; he is much more interested in what we do – in varying circumstances – in order to learn, argue, and convince others.

Summing up, in *Image* and *Representation* van Fraassen offers a whole range of elements that naturally befit a "Wittgensteinian Kantianism." The position is Kantian in its emphasis on the "construction" and "creation" of phenomenal worlds through processes of *representation*. And it is Wittgensteinian insofar as van Fraassen recognizes the priority of pragmatics over semantics and of local and indexical elements over stable and autonomous (mathematical) structures. Insofar as it makes sense to speak of an "apriori" at all, it is neither atemporal (as in Kant) nor a time-honored historical resource (as in Friedman). It consists, rather, of interpretations produced by historically situated agents, acting to further both theoretical and other aims and goals. This clearly falls into my "model" for relativism as outlined in Section 2.

Stances

In *Stance*, van Fraassen aims to show that empiricism is best understood as a stance. Since the nineteenth century, empiricism has often been summed up in the dogma "DOGMA" ...

---

[139] Ibid., loc. 1176–1828.   [140] Ibid., loc. 1,784.

(DOGMA) "experience is the one and only source of information."[141]

For van Fraassen this is not just historically inaccurate – self-declared empiricists have always had a much wider range of commitments – but it is also unhelpful for demarcating empiricism from its main rival: metaphysics.

Empiricists (a) want to be able to dismiss metaphysics *tout court* and (b) do not want to be drawn into protracted debates over the pros and cons of specific metaphysical proposals. Empiricists – or at least naturalist empiricists – also demand (c) that philosophical theses must be empirical hypotheses and that as such (d) they deserve to be extensively tested by reasoning based on empirical observation and experimentation. Unfortunately, (a)–(d) do not fit together with rendering empiricism primarily according to DOGMA. First, if DOGMA defines empiricism, and empiricism is the opposite of metaphysics, then metaphysics can be summed up as the negation of DOGMA. Second, if DOGMA is an empirical hypothesis (as per (c)), then so is the negation of DOGMA. Third, as empirical hypotheses, both DOGMA and its negation deserve their long day in the court of empirical tests (as per (d)). But then, fourth, empiricists cannot summarily reject metaphysics (pace (a)), and they have to enter into detailed investigations of specific metaphysical proposals (pace (b)).

Reinterpreting empiricism as a stance avoids these problems. The clash between empiricism and metaphysics is not a conflict between empirical hypotheses; it is a clash between sets of virtues, values, emotions, preferences, and policies (=VVEPPs). Since none of these VVEPPs are empirical hypotheses, they do not get checked in the normal ways of empirical science. Moreover, whereas empiricism is – or so van Fraassen suggests – the embodiment of many of the VVEPPs characteristic of empirical science, metaphysics is not. And this allows empiricists to dismiss metaphysics out of hand. Of course, empiricists and metaphysicians differ in their beliefs and dogmas, too. But since the metaphysicians' beliefs are motivated by a problematic value orientation, they do not require – for the stance-empiricist – careful scrutiny. Some of the key VVEPPs of empiricism-as-stance are "disvaluing of explanation by postulate" (i.e. rejecting the postulation of unobservable entities), "calling us back to experience, ... rebellion against theory, ideals of epistemic rationality, ... admiration for science, and ... an idea of rationality that does not bar disagreement." "None" of these "attitudes" can be equated with beliefs.[142]

There are several relativist motifs in van Fraassen's account of stances. One is that adopting a stance has an element of "conversion": "Being or becoming an empiricist [is] similar or analogous to conversion to a cause, a religion, an ideology, to capitalism or to socialism."[143] While we can try to *persuade* others

---

[141] van Fraassen, *Empirical Stance*, p. 43.   [142] Ibid., p. 47.   [143] Ibid., p. 61.

to adopt our stances, we cannot *rationally compel* them to switch. This is precisely because stances are in good part defined by VVEPPs. This does not make the adoption of stances "irrational" but points to limitations of rational debate. Debates over values, emotions, or preferences can never be as clear-cut as arguments over beliefs within one and the same stance can be.

Stance also harbors a second relativist idea, to wit, "the virtue [empiricists] see in an idea of rationality that does not bar disagreement."[144] This refers to a form of "permissivism": the rejection of the thought that there is one, and only one, rational response to a given body of evidence. van Fraassen's permissivism is easy to rationalize from within his general views of data models: there is always more than one rational technique to model a given set of data; there is more than one rational strategy to construct surface models out of data models; and, thus, there is more than one procedure to turn data into evidence for a given theoretical model. Moreover, van Fraassen's discussion naturally invites the thought that relativism is itself something of a stance: the relativist is committed to tolerating, permitting, and cherishing fundamental disagreements in both philosophy and science, disagreements that can rationally persist – until and unless one side "converts" to the other side.

Voluntarism

"Voluntarism" is the name for a theory of rationality that gives *the will* a central place. At issue is the right to choose one's (epistemic) values and convictions, and thereby – at least in part – determine the rational ideals by which one wishes to be judged.

Stance tells us that the fundamental norm of rationality is to "avoid self-sabotage": to avoid reasoning that – even by our own lights – prevents us from reaching our goals. van Fraassen takes this to mean that we must avoid logical inconsistency and probabilistic incoherence, and thus commit to "principles of rationality": that is, deductive logic, the theory of probability, and the practical syllogism.[145] Call these "principles of rationality" "rationality in the narrow sense."

van Fraassen credits William James[146] with the insight that rationality in the narrow sense underdetermines many of our epistemic choices. (Rudolf Carnap's "Lambda-parameter" for degree of aversion to risk and Carnap's "Principle of Tolerance"[147] are also important here.) Simply put, we each have to set out "risk-quotients"; for example, do we primarily seek to avoid false positives or false negatives; do we set the hurdle for justification high or low? We all do so,

---

[144] Ibid., p. 47.   [145] Ibid., pp. 88, 224.   [146] James, *The Will to Believe*.
[147] Carnap, *Logical Syntax*; Carnap, *Inductive Methods*.

be it reflectively or spontaneously, with regard to changing circumstances or not. Rationality in the narrow sense does not come with criteria that would give a unique answer. This is where VVEPPs once more become important. We have to decide, say, whether in general, or in a given situation, the potential harm from false positives is greater than the potential harm from false negatives. Deciding this question involves value judgements. This suggests that stances are not just important in "metaphilosophy." They are also significant for understanding our choices and commitments as epistemic and moral agents.

The most plausible interpretation of these ideas is to attribute to van Fraassen a two-layered conception of rationality. There is rationality in the *narrow* sense, and there is rationality in the *broad* sense. The first is constituted by principles of rationality (logic, theory of probability) and the latter is constituted additionally by our VVEPPs. The former is minimalist-normative-prescriptive, and the latter is expansive-axiological-voluntarist. The former is rationally without alternative; the latter comes in a number of forms. The former leaves no room for relativism; the latter clearly does.

Revolutions

van Fraassen argues in favor of his conception of rationality by invoking Kuhnian revolutions. van Fraassen accepts Kuhn's idea that the relationship between successive paradigms, P_1 and P_2, is such that followers of P_1 cannot but look upon P_2 as "literally absurd, incoherent, obviously false." Nevertheless, looking back from P_2 on P_1, when P_1 has been reinterpreted in light of P_2, P_1 is often recognized as a partial truth.[148] The notion that Newtonian mechanics is a special case of relativistic mechanics is a case in point. van Fraassen adds that P_2 frequently results in the discovery of *ambiguities* in P_1. The textbook example is the distinction between "proper mass," "gravitational mass," and "inertial mass" in Einstein.[149]

van Fraassen is particularly interested in how the new paradigm can become a "live" option. His answer lies with "emotions" or similar "impulses." *Stance* uses Kafka's *Metamorphosis* as an example. Gregor Samsa is an ordinary young bureaucrat, living with his parents and sister Greta. One night, in his sleep, he turns into a gigantic beetle, unable to communicate with humans. His family are shocked. At first they try to continue with normal life, treating the beetle as Gregor. Alas, this quickly turns out to be impossible; Gregor-the-beetle's needs and actions are simply too opaque, unpredictable, and absurd. Amidst the growing desperation, Greta suffers a mental breakdown. This "impulse" changes the way the family perceive the beetle: not as Gregor but as a creepy

---

[148] van Fraassen, *Empirical Stance*, p. 71.   [149] Ibid., p. 113.

animal that has destroyed their son. This new perception then justifies killing the insect.[150]

The change in the family's thinking before and after Greta's breakdown can also be captured in the following terms – which fit with two further claims van Fraassen makes about scientific revolutions.[151] First, throughout the whole episode the parents and Greta stick to one and the same rule:

(PROTECT) Protect your family members.

But before Greta's breakdown the rule was interpreted or used in a "conservative" way, in that the domain of the rule was not changed when Gregor turned into a beetle. After Greta's emotional outburst, PROTECT was rendered in a "revolutionary" manner: the domain of the rule was changed so as to exclude Gregor from its domain. Put differently, and this is the second claim, the shift in the two readings of PROTECT can be understood as the increasing realization that "family member" is ambiguous between . . .

(WIDE) family member with the mental life of a human being, whatever their outward appearance; and

(NARROW) family member with the outward appearance *and* inner life of a human being.

Ultimately, Gregor's family switched from WIDE to NARROW.

In the case of scientific revolutions, van Fraassen explains the change in the use of a rule of method as follows. His example is the empiricist stricture . . .

(SE) "*Sola experientia!*" (Roughly: Let sensory experience be the only yardstick.)

Defenders of the old paradigm, P_1, insist that SE provides a justification for P_1 and that P_1 does not go beyond experience in illegitimate ways. In other words, the proponents of P_1 use SE in a *conservative* way. The revolutionaries promoting P_2 make the same claim for P_2, *mutatis mutandis*. At the same time, they claim to be able to identify metaphysical baggage in P_1, excess structure that is not licensed by experience. Think of Newton's notion of absolute space. The defenders of P_2 thus employ SE in a "revolutionary" manner.[152]

van Fraassen takes his account of scientific revolutions to support his voluntarism. The crucial test for epistemologies, according to *Stance*, is whether or not they can safeguard the rationality of science and progress while accepting as inevitable the elements of impulse and conversion at the very core of scientific revolutions. van Fraassen divides epistemologies into two categories: "objectifying" and

---

[150] Ibid., p. 106.   [151] Ibid., ch. 4.   [152] Ibid.

"voluntarist." The paradigmatic case of the former category is "naturalized epistemology." Its proponents see epistemology as closely intertwined with psychology and other cognitive sciences.

Voluntarist epistemology is much more minimalist: it does not aim for proximity to contemporary sciences, and it restricts itself to a small set of principles (think subjective Bayesian epistemology). Voluntarist epistemology does better than objectifying epistemology for three reasons. First, its narrow conception of rationality is prescriptive-evaluative rather than descriptive-explanatory.[153] This cuts the ties to prevalent scientific paradigms. Second, the principles of rationality constitute a minimalist conception: they therefore leave the choice between the old and the new paradigm underdetermined. And, third, epistemic voluntarism gives VVEPPs – including emotion and similar impulses – a legitimate place in our epistemic life. Although the shift from one paradigm to another will typically be tantamount to a shift from one stance to another, the "conversion" involved in both shifts can be influenced by appeal to VVEPPs.

van Fraassen's account of scientific revolutions can also be read as support for some other of his central tenets. First, the insistence upon *Sola experientia!* as a central rule of theory- and paradigm-choice is, of course, part and parcel of constructive empiricism. Second, the suggestion that scientific revolutions involve reinterpretations of received rules or rule-formulations is naturally seen in light of what I earlier called the "indexicalism" of *Representation*. And third, van Fraassen renders progress without reference to truth. Instead, he speaks of progress as consisting of the removing of ambiguities and the reconceptualizing of the old and the new in such a way that the old appears as a special case of the new. Clearly, given the indexicality of theory-interpretation, there will always be multiple ways to "discover ambiguities" and multiple ways to render the old as a precursor of the new.

Voluntarism and Relativism

The *Stance*-position falls into the relativistic spectrum of Section 2. Judgements are relative to stances/paradigms (DEPENDENCE); there are multiple stances/paradigms in science (PLURALITY), at least diachronically; different such stances/paradigms are sometimes incompatible or incommensurable (CONFLICT); the shift from one stance/paradigm to another can have the character of a conversion (CONVERSION); and the arguments defending specific stances/paradigms are invariably local (SYMMETRY as LOCALITY).

The *Stance*-account also coheres with the relativism of *Image* and *Representation*. In particular, and pace Teller,[154] the model-centric approach

---

[153] Ibid.　　[154] Teller, "Idealizations."

to theories does not jar with the Kuhnian account of scientific revolutions. Sometimes the new paradigm simply comes with new "model building tool kits" that replace the old paradigm and its models wholesale.[155] In other cases, some models of the old paradigm are preserved within the new paradigm; obviously, some Newtonian models survive to this day. Remember that van Fraassen explicitly allows that elements of the old paradigm can retrospectively be recognized – or better, reconstructed – as special cases of the new. Clearly, the Newtonian models still used today are no longer interpreted with Newtonian language and metaphysics.

Moreover, the *Stance*-account fits together with both the earlier emphasis on "hermeneutic circles," "anthropocentrism," the idea of "objectivity" as a stance-internal standard, and historicist-relativist Kantianism. The last element is the most obvious. van Fraassen's history of science exemplifies this very idea: there is no standpoint outside historically changing and contingent stances/paradigms. And there is no element in the *Stance*-theory that would take us beyond the limits of the human. Even the principles of rationality are not absolutely binding, but binding for creatures with our specific dangers of falling into self-sabotage.

Stance was written *before Representation*, but here too the various theoretical elements fit together coherently. Indexicality, with its emphasis on local, contextual, variable, and contingent agency, further supports the idea that scientific crises of confidence can be resolved in different ways and guided by different values, emotions, and preferences. And the *Representation*-arguments against structural and perspectival realism undergird the Kuhnian and van-Fraassenian skepticism about getting ever closer to truth.

Critical Discussion

I now turn from exposition and explanation to critical evaluation. In developing critical perspectives on van Fraassen's relativism, I shall use some of the resources introduced in the first two sections.

Stances

Stances are an intriguing addition to the arsenal of the historian of philosophy and of the philosopher, historian, and sociologist of science. And stances come with a novel template for thinking about relativism.

To start with the history of philosophy, many "isms" are fruitfully taken as bundles of VVEPPs. The epistemological anarchism briefly summarized in

---

[155] van Fraassen, *Representation*, loc. 248.

Section 3 is a case in point.[156] In Section 2, I suggested that relativism itself could perhaps be viewed as a stance, since most relativists are rebelling against absolutist forms of metaphysics, epistemology, or ethics; oppose intellectual imperialism; and value epistemic humility or tolerance. Or, to mention a couple of German intellectual movements (with which I am familiar[157]), take "Neo-Kantianism"[158] or "Phenomenology"[159] of the nineteenth and early twentieth centuries. The key protagonists were united in a "rebellion" against the increasing influence, in the humanities, of naturalistic and natural-scientific modes of thought; an admiration for Kant's philosophy; or a concern to protect German culture against the rise of relativist-historist forms of analysis. At the same time, the two schools differed with regard to their research policies: many Neo-Kantians sought to emulate Kant's methodology, while many phenomenologists aimed to take their lead from Franz Brentano's or Edmund Husserl's analyses of mental content.

Admittedly, the existence of stances will be news more to philosophers than to historians. The latter are already open to the possibility that intellectual movements are held together as much by VVEPPs as by doctrines or beliefs. It is also worth adding that – when it comes to understanding the unity of a philosophical tradition – it is difficult, if not impossible, to decide whether the primary unifying link is VVEPPs or beliefs.

Determining the relative importance of VVEPPs and beliefs is also difficult in the sciences. That VVEPPs play crucial roles in science has been amply documented in feminist, historical, and sociological scholarship. Kuhn, for instance, draws attention to the values of accuracy, consistency, scope, simplicity, and fruitfulness; and the feminist Helen Longino campaigns instead, or additionally, for "empirical adequacy," "novelty (of theoretical framework)," "heterogeneity," "reciprocity of interaction," "alleviation of human needs," or "decentralization of power."[160] If "stances" are to be more than just a fancy new terminology for familiar phenomena, we need to be told how they are to interact with other analytic categories like "paradigm" (as exemplars and as disciplinary matrices), "research tradition," or "school." Further reflections on this theme might well lead to a better understanding of relativism. CONFLICT, PLURALITY, and CONVERSION seem easier to make sense of when it comes to values and preferences than in application to "principles" or "practices." After all, in our twenty-first-century multicultural societies, we all have (had) plenty of experience with fundamental disagreements over values.

---

[156] See also Kusch, "Epistemological Anarchism."   [157] Cf. Kusch, *Psychologism*.
[158] Cf. Köhnke, *The Rise of Neo-Kantianism*.
[159] Cf. Spiegelberg, *The Phenomenological Movement*.   [160] Longino, "Values, Heuristics."

Objectifying and Voluntarist Epistemology

van Fraassen's distinction between objectifying and voluntarist epistemology introduces a new dividing line in epistemology. The distinction covers conflicting answers to two different questions:

(a) Should epistemology be closely intertwined with, and thus build upon, the sciences of the day?

(b) Should (core, universal, absolute) epistemology have a wide scope; that is, should it leave few, if any, areas of the epistemic realm unconstrained?

Objectifying epistemology responds with "yes" to both questions; voluntarist epistemology with "no" to both. Surprisingly, van Fraassen seems not to have noticed that there are two further options: "yes" to (a) and "no" to (b); and "no" to (a) and "yes" to (b). In other words, an epistemology entangled with the sciences but with a narrow scope; and an epistemology distant from the sciences but with a wide scope. The latter conception is close to mainstream analytic epistemology (in the tradition of Chisholm and Gettier); the former is near to naturalized epistemology (in the tradition of Goldman, Quine, or SSK). van Fraassen's oversight matters for his argument. The fact that objectifying epistemology fails the litmus-test of saving the rationality of scientific revolutions does not speak uniquely in favor of voluntarist epistemology. Mainstream epistemology or narrow-scope naturalized epistemology might also make the cut.

As it stands, the content of van Fraassen's voluntarist epistemology is unclear. He first introduces voluntarism as a view about rationality, to wit, that the latter is fully captured by deductive logic, probability theory, and the practical syllogism. Taken at face value, these are not epistemic principles. Are we to construct voluntarist epistemology in analogy to voluntarism about rationality? Are there "narrow" and "wide" epistemic rationality, such that the former is universal and absolute, and the latter local and relative? How are we to draw this distinction? Perhaps existing work in the "genealogy of knowledge" could be useful here.[161]

van Fraassen deserves credit for reflecting on the role of epistemologies in scientific revolutions. It seems eminently plausible that, when such revolutions occur, epistemology changes too. As we saw in Section 3, Feyerabend pointed out as much concerning the Copernican Revolution. And yet, even during the Copernican Revolution, many epistemic practices or principles remained stable. Changes concerned questions like: who is a reliable testifier; are instruments like the telescope essential for producing knowledge; what are the standards of

---

[161] See Craig, *Knowledge and the State of Nature*.

scientific proof; or are biblical texts literally true? Other epistemic notions did not change; for example, epistemic notions about the perceptual appearance of close medium-size objects in broad daylight.

Additionally, it seems a fair guess that the epistemic ideas prevalent in a given historical period do not form a coherent whole. Different coexisting groups differ in some of their epistemic ideas, and even the epistemic conceptions of one and the same group often contain contradictions. The epistemic disunity and the uneven effects of revolutions on epistemologies further weaken van Fraassen's argument for voluntarist epistemology. This is because van Fraassen's argument presupposes that scientific revolutions involve a clash between two unified epistemologies whose defenders cannot but see each other as wholly irrational. It is to avoid this result that, according to van Fraassen, we need voluntarist epistemology with its minimalist commitment. But the mere fact that *some parts* of an objectifying epistemology are incompatible with a given revolutionary change need not result in the respective epistemologists' overall verdict that this revolutionary change is irrational.

Moderate or Radical Voluntarism

van Fraassen's conception of rationality is layered: the lower stratum consists of universal or absolute principles of rationality and the higher stratum of the relative and variable VVEPPs. Narrow rationality is defined by the lower stratum; wide rationality is a combination of narrow rationality and a specific choice amongst VVEPPs. We can put pressure on this theory by noting that absolute principles of rationality are definitionally interdependent with values: no-self-sabotage, consistency, and coherence are values captured or secured by the principles. van Fraassen takes these values to be without alternative and gives special weight to consistency.[162] Obviously, there are alternatives to this conception. Relatively close to van Fraassen is the later Kuhn,[163] who speaks of "shared epistemic values" (of accuracy, consistency, scope, simplicity, and fruitfulness) as the rational backbone of theory or paradigm choice. Still, Kuhn also notes that different scientists rank and interpret these values in different ways. This makes consistency part of a complicated mix of values rather than the absolute touchstone. It is not obvious that one can subsume Kuhn's account under van Fraassen's stratified picture.

Other philosophers also differ from van Fraassen when it comes to thinking about rationality. van Fraassen recognizes as much when he mentions Graham Priest:

---

[162] van Fraassen, "Replies," 184–5.   [163] Kuhn, *Essential Tension.*

> What if I detect a straightforward contradiction in someone's beliefs, con-
> clude that he has sabotaged himself in the management of his opinions, and he
> turns out to be Graham Priest? Priest happily admits to believing that certain
> contradictions are or may be true.[164]

van Fraassen responds by saying that Priest's logic is "quite different from the one most familiar to us" and that evolutionary arguments might ultimately speak against it.[165] I am not convinced. Priest argues that consistency is a matter of degree and must always be weighed against other cognitive values such as "simplicity," "unity," "explanatory power," or "parsimony."[166] It is not obvious that and how evolutionary arguments could work against Priest's proposal.

A further alternative to van Fraassen's treating consistency and other traditional epistemic values as sacrosanct comes from feminist philosophy. I have already mentioned Longino's case for values such as empirical adequacy, novelty (of theoretical framework), heterogeneity, reciprocity of interaction, alleviation of human needs, or decentralization of power.[167] Longino is adamant that novelty (of theoretical framework) "is contrary to the value of consistency with theories in other domains as described by Kuhn . . . or . . . conservatism (that is, preserving as much of one's prior belief set as possible)."[168] She also insists that "the normative claim" of a given set of values "is limited to the community sharing the primary goal."[169] One possible such goal is "[dismantling] . . . the oppression and subordination of women."[170] Feyerabend would, of course, be happy to side with Priest and Longino. *Against Method* extensively rails against the so-called "consistency condition," that is, the idea that a new scientific theory must be consistent with existing theories or observations.[171] Feyerabend also proclaims that "there is not a single science, or other form of life that is useful, progressive as well as in agreement with logical demands."[172]

These alternatives to van Fraassen reveal that there are two ways to think about voluntarism: van Fraassen's *moderate* position, and Longino's and Priest's *radical* version. Moderate voluntarism takes certain values to be universal and without alternative; radical voluntarism does not. This is not the place to decide the conflict between these two options. But it is an issue constructive empiricists and epistemic voluntarists need to address. Be this as it may, the fact that van Fraassen's voluntarism is *moderate* rather than *radical* does not mean that it is outside the relativistic spectrum: it just shows that van Fraassen's relativism is limited. There is for him no relativism concerning

---

[164] van Fraassen, "Replies," 184.   [165] Ibid., 185.   [166] Priest, *Doubt Truth*, p. 123.
[167] Longino, "Values, Heuristics."   [168] Ibid., 70.   [169] Ibid., 79.
[170] Ibid., 77. In using Longino against van Fraassen, I am following Okruhlik, "van Fraassen's Philosophy" and "Science, Sex, and Pictures."
[171] Feyerabend, *Against Method*, p. 35.   [172] Ibid., pp. 258–9.

narrow rationality, the minimalist core of canons of rationality. But relativism is accepted as soon as we step beyond this core and pick our stances. In other words, relativism is correct as far as wide rationality is concerned.

Scientific Revolutions and Pluralism

van Fraassen paints the following rough picture of the unfolding of a scientific revolution: problems mount for the old paradigm/stance; scientists increasingly doubt that they can make it work; they fall into epistemic despair; they encounter a new – initially absurd – paradigm/stance; and then an emotion-like impulse enables them to reconceptualize this alternative as a live option.

One problem with this picture is that it says little about pluralism and discipline-splitting as responses to anomalies. That said, there is nothing in van Fraassen's position that actually rules out pluralism in either a descriptive or a normative form. And, as I hinted earlier, perhaps it can even be said that the theory of stances and voluntarism actually gives some support to pluralism.

Impulses

If stances are an essential part, or complement, of scientific paradigms, then they likely play a crucial role in scientific revolutions. van Fraassen's emphasis on "impulses" as instrumental in turning an absurd into a "live option" is in line with this expectation. After all, his only example of such impulses is emotions, and emotions are part of the VVEPPs-bundles. Perhaps the right way to flesh out van Fraassen's idea is precisely to highlight the role of VVEPPs in revolutionary change.

As it stands, the "impulses" needed for scientific revolutions are specified functionally: they are whatever it needs to constitute live options for theory choice. But is it obvious that this functional role can only be filled by VVEPPs? I do not think so. Remember as an example Greta of the Samsa family. Did it really need an emotion to make her and her parents realize that the beetle was replacing rather than embodying Gregor? Could this not also have been achieved by, say, a philosophical argument that undermines belief in personal identity across change of species?

Incommensurability, Absurdity, Rationality

In his thinking about incommensurability, van Fraassen is indebted to Feyerabend. As far as semantic incommensurability is concerned, van Fraassen applauds Feyerabend's one-time use of a Homeric example.[173]

---

[173] Feyerabend, *Conquest of Abundance.*

Feyerabend identifies an instance of a radical conceptual change in the *Iliad*: the shift from equating "being honorable" with "being honored by one's society," to recognizing that these two states can come apart. When Achilles first insisted on the difference, his interlocutors, as Homer puts it, "fell silent, for he had spoken in stunning ways."[174] To bring about his desired conceptual change, Achilles drew on the inherent plasticity of language as well as language-users' willingness to tolerate temporary situations of incomprehension.[175] Achilles also cleverly invoked parallels. He pointed out a gap between "being honored by the Gods" and "being honored by one's society." Once his audience had been reminded of this gap, they found it easier to recognize a similar hiatus between the second expression and "being honorable."[176] Feyerabend sees similar linguistic tricks on display when scientists try to impose meaning-change in their communities.[177] van Fraassen agrees.

Feyerabend's and van Fraassen's account of radical conceptual shifts is importantly different from Kuhn's in that Feyerabend (at least sometimes) and van Fraassen (regularly) put greater stress on linguistic change as an *intentional action*. Incommensurability and commensurability are situations that scientists actively either try to bring about or try to prevent. This focus tallies nicely with historical work by Mario Biagioli, according to which Aristotelian natural philosophers had every (political) reason to protest the alleged incomprehensibility of Copernican mathematical astronomers – and vice versa.[178]

Feyerabend is van Fraassen's interlocutor also when it comes to methodological incommensurability. Earlier, we saw that van Fraassen sees advocates of the old and the new paradigm (P_1 and P_2) as divided by two radically different renderings of (SE) "*sola experientia!*": the proponents of P_1 use SE *conservatively* so as to defend the strength of their theories; the supporters of P_2 employ SE in a *revolutionary* way in order to undermine P_1. van Fraassen's discussion is geared to combining radical change in the methodological use of SE with a certain stability of content: an empiricist commitment at the heart of science. The emphasis on stability is missing, however, in the text by Feyerabend – "Classical Empiricism"[179] – upon which van Fraassen purports to build. Feyerabend is arguing that the early-modern SE, like its contemporary "*sola scriptura!*," was "vacuous."[180] It had a clear meaning only for those who already thought that experience (or scripture) was important; only for those who rendered experience (or scripture) in similar ways; and only for those who concurred on how experience (or scripture) could be the source of knowledge.

---

[174] Ibid., p. 19.   [175] Ibid., p. 32.   [176] Ibid., p. 36.
[177] Feyerabend, *Against Method*, p. 270.   [178] Biagioli, "Anthropology."
[179] Feyerabend, "Empiricism."   [180] Ibid., p. 41.

But a community who agreed on so much did not actually need the slogan. Accordingly, "it [was] no more than a party line."[181]

Feyerabend continues by analyzing Newton's style of reasoning. Feyerabend is particularly intrigued by one particular strategy in Newton. In a first phase, a scientific proposal is made familiar by being repeated over and over again. And in a second phase, the very familiarity of the proposal is invoked "as if it were an additional source of support." As Feyerabend has it, this strategy is "not different from political propaganda."[182]

van Fraassen wishes to go along with Feyerabend only part of the way. He wishes to resist the reduction of SE to a "vacuous" slogan. But it is difficult to recognize by what argument van Fraassen has achieved his goal, especially since his own indexicalism seems to lend support to Feyerabend's rather than his own position.

Has van Fraassen succeeded in securing the rationality of scientific revolutions? This depends, of course, on how we understand scientific rationality. If we use Michael Friedman's[183] criteria, then van Fraassen has failed. There is nothing in van Fraassen that would support the idea that existing science is "an approximation to a final, ideal community of inquiry."[184] Although van Fraassen has not discussed Friedman's *Dynamics of Reason* in print, he has signaled sympathies for Marc Lange's critical essay-review, which undermines many of Friedman's factual historical claims meant to support the normative and metaphysical superstructure.[185] Lange shows, for instance, that philosophy did not have the crucial role of procuring "inter-paradigm rationality."

We can also assess van Fraassen's attempt to "save" the rationality of scientific revolutions independently of comparisons with Friedman or Feyerabend. First, it is questionable whether van Fraassen's theorizing is successful even on its own terms. How can the key to saving the rationality of scientific revolutions be a "brute" cause or impulse? It may well be that retrospectively all will look rational. But is this enough for comfort? After all, retrospectively all might look rational even to converts to cults.

Second, in his attempt to save rationality across revolutions, van Fraassen reduces rationality and epistemology to a small set of prescriptions. The less content to rationality or epistemology, the thought seems to be, the less there is for a revolution to contradict. Alas, this strategy jars with the goals of the philosophy of science. Do we really want an epistemology that is so minimalist-prescriptive as to not connect up with our best science? How could it not be

---

[181] Ibid., p. 51.   [182] Ibid.   [183] Friedman, *Dynamics*; Friedman, "Extending the Dynamics."
[184] Ibid., loc. 1391–5.   [185] Lange, "Review"; van Fraassen (in conversation).

connected up? Isn't the acceptance of every methodology always the acceptance of certain epistemic inductive principles or practices? van Fraassen faces
a dilemma here: if he makes epistemology thick enough (high-resolution
enough) that it can say something illuminating about scientific work – and
this is clearly something van Fraassen wants – then it will change when science
changes: and the change might well look "irrational" or "absurd." If he makes
epistemology thin enough (low-resolution enough) that it remains unchanged
across scientific revolutions, then it will be unable to say much of interest about
scientific work. Or, to put it still differently: Do we really want to sacrifice the
project of a high-resolution epistemology of science on the altar of the credo
"rationality does not change"? How reassuring is it to be told, *forte voce*,
"rationality is stable" followed by the addition, *sotto voce*, "of course, only in
a very minimalist sense of rational"?

Finally, perhaps van Fraassen is misled by the assumption that the best
argument in favor of voluntarism in the theory of rationality and in epistemology has to run through a certain understanding of scientific revolutions. Why
does the argument have to be so complicated? Are there no other ways to
motivate skepticism vis-à-vis naturalized epistemology; and are there no other
means to defend the idea of a narrow-scope conception of rationality and
epistemology? Why aren't the historical and cultural differences in what has
been, and is, regarded as rational and (epistemically) justified good enough?

Boghossian's Objections

How does van Fraassen's relativism fare against Boghossian's general objections to relativism (as I have canvassed these in Section 2)? To begin with, I take
it to be obvious that van Fraassen's position is not a case of "vulgar" relativism;
there is no commitment to EQUAL VALIDITY anywhere in his oeuvre. As
concerns Boghossian's two master-arguments on behalf of relativism, it is
worth pointing out that neither of them appears in *Stance*, *Image* or
Representation. In van Fraassen, relativism is advanced on much more general
grounds: by emphasizing our limitations as "measuring devices" shaped by the
contingencies of evolution; by highlighting the essential locality and indexicality of scientific work; or by drawing attention to fundamental change in
science. To be sure, such change involves transformations in many fundamental
epistemic principles. But such transformations do not fit into the format
Boghossian employs in discussing the case of Bellarmine.

Is van Fraassen's relativism self-refuting? Surely not, if the self-refutation
argument is premised on the thought that relativist and absolutist belong to two
different epistemic communities. Even if we follow my suggestion and treat

relativism and absolutism as two different philosophical stances, we do not have to rule out that relativists or absolutists can try to argue their case on the basis of principles and values endorsed by both. Needless to say, there is no guarantee that they will succeed, but that is par for the course for all value-based philosophical disagreements. Nor is van Fraassen committed to the view that the absolutist is "epistemically blameless" if she so chooses her epistemic standards that relativism turns out unjustified. Epistemic voluntarism allows us leeway in choosing our values. But it is no general license for picking our values without reasonably compelling considerations.

Recall Boghossian's doubts about relativist "double-think." The relativist wants to be able to pronounce other sets of standards (=S) mistaken. But she also wishes to maintain that her own S is not absolutely correct, or closer to absolute correctness than other S. As Boghossian has it, these two goals do not fit together. Without a commitment to our S's being at least approximately absolutely correct, we have no right to favor it over others. Moreover, the problem cannot be avoided by distinguishing between two perspectives: the committed perspective, in which we treat our S as absolute, and the meta-perspective that treats all S as equally relative. This would result in "serious cognitive dissonance."

van Fraassen does not see the problem. At one stage he writes: "I remain convinced that genuine, conscious reflection on alternative beliefs, orientations, values – in an open and undogmatic spirit – does not automatically undermine one's own commitments."[186] This is, of course, true when formulated in this very general way. But what should we say about a situation in which the "alternative beliefs, orientations, values" are those of another stance?

van Fraassen's response should be twofold. If the other stance violates rationality in the narrow sense, then it can be dismissed. After all, van Fraassen treats rationality in the narrow sense as something absolute. A different answer is needed for cases where the conflict concerns differences in VVEPPs. van Fraassen's permissivism and historicism make the following reply natural. The fact that another stance is committed to other VVEPPs does not give me reason to feel undermined in my commitment to my stance. I can recognize that there are (narrowly) rational alternatives to my VVEPPs, alternatives permitted by narrow rationality. Those are questions over which (narrowly) rational people can disagree. Since there is no absolute right or wrong regarding VVEPPs, there is no reason to be worried about the lack of an absolute anchor for our own choices concerning them. At the same time, it is a mistake to think, like Boghossian, that a "mere" relative, contingent anchor

---

[186] van Fraassen, "Stance and Rationality," 156.

is no anchor at all. To claim as much is simply to insist that absolutism must be right.

So much for the reply that a moderate epistemic voluntarist might give. What about the radical epistemic voluntarist? She would not be able to invoke an absolute narrow form of rationality. Still, the radical can generalize the argument of the moderate. Boghossian assumes that without a commitment to an absolute standard for S, all S are equal. But that is precisely what the relativist denies. Given van Fraassen's occasional allusions to Sartrean existentialism, we might put the idea as follows. We find ourselves "always already" "thrown" into certain stances. Over time we learn to modify and improve them – by the lights drawn from these very stances. But we can never redesign them from scratch or measure them against an ideal. When we encounter genuine alternatives to our own stance, we can sometimes come to understand their motivations and inner structure, even without making them our own. We can also come to dismiss aspects of them. These dismissals are relative to our stance and thus contingent on our particular history and context. Recognizing this contingency may well make us less "absolutist" in our verdicts on these alternatives; but it does not commit us to renouncing judgement altogether. Perhaps the radical voluntarism can also take a leaf out of van Fraassen's psychologistic anthropocentrism (from *Image*) and insist that – although there is no absolute set of standards – there still are standards frequently found in humans, based on our common evolutionary history.

If the argument of the last two paragraphs is sound, then epistemic voluntarism can avoid Boghossian's double-think objection. No doubt, the moderate version of voluntarism – that is, van Fraassen's own version – has an easier task here than the radical variant. Still, the moderate version is prima facie threatened by Boghossian's criticism of "absolute relativism," forms of relativism that work with a combination of absolute and relativist principles. van Fraassen clearly does: narrow rationality is absolute. Recall that Boghossian has two concerns: first, that in allowing for absolute principles the relativist loses her strongest card, to wit, worries over how absolutes fit into the world and how they can be grasped by creatures like us; and, second, that in accepting some absolute principles the relativist needs a good answer to the question why there aren't even more.

I suspect van Fraassen would agree with both of Boghossian's observations concerning absolute relativism. But this agreement does not constitute a fatal admission of failure. All Boghossian shows here is that the absolute relativist is – as far as absolute principles are concerned – in exactly the same boat as the full-blown absolutist like Boghossian. Both need to tell a convincing story about how absolutes can be known by creatures like us, and both need to tell us why some, rather than all, principles are absolute. After all, even the most radical absolutist won't declare *all* principles to be absolute.

Finally, Boghossian insists that what variation we find regarding our epistemic standards can be explained on the grounds that our absolute principles leave us some leeway. This explanation is better, and simpler, than the explanation in terms of altogether different, alternative sets of principles. Again, I do not think that this objection cuts much ice against the moderate voluntarist. Indeed, van Fraassen's position is very much a variant of Boghossian's proposal. Narrow rationality leaves us leeway in picking our (bundles of) VVEPPs. Boghossian and van Fraassen might still differ on the extent of the leeway. But this further question cannot be decided in the abstract.

The radical voluntarist must give a different answer. She has to emphasize that Boghossian's comment does no more than highlight one possible way of accounting for the variation in standards. Whether this really is the better or simpler explanation is far from clear. Boghossian assumes that postulating absolutes is simpler than restricting oneself to relative, empirical, contingent phenomena. But this assumption is exactly what divides absolutists and relativists.

Summary

This section was long and complex. It seems, therefore, imperative to summarize its main findings in a succinct form.

(1) There are a number of relativism-related motifs in *Image*: anti-realism; an emphasis on scientific work as "construction rather than discovery"; the denial of a *punctum archimedis* concerning observability; anthropologism; historicism; and the rejection of objectivity as a neutral standard.

(2) The central relativist *topos* in *Representation* is what I called "indexicalism": the notion that all aspects of scientific representation have to be analyzed in terms of local and varying goals; individual and collective agency; interests and values; and conceptual resources and interpretations. I called the resulting position a "Wittgensteinian Kantianism."

(3) van Fraassen's relativism is most clearly developed in *Stance* and related writings. One key element is the idea of a stance qua bundle of VVEPPs, and in particular the thought that it needs something of a "conversion" to adopt a new stance. I suggested that relativism, too, can be looked upon as a stance.

(4) The most significant relativist element of *Stance* is voluntarism, that is, a layered conception of rationality: the lower stratum is, or should be,

shared by all humans and specified by the criterion of "no-self-sabotage." The upper stratum consists of epistemic and other values that vary with culture (individual and collective). The adoption of a particular form of the upper stratum is constrained (but not uniquely determined) by the lower stratum.

(5) The layered conception of rationality is needed to "safeguard" the continuity of rationality across scientific revolutions. Scientific revolutions involve reinterpretations of epistemic rules, emotions, or other impulses as well as meaning-change.

(6) The conception of *Stance* fits with the model of relativism presented in Section 2.

(7) My critical assessment of *Stance* sought to establish the following conclusions:

(a) "Stance" is indeed a valuable addition to the repertoire of the historian of ideas.

(b) The distinction between objectifying and voluntarist epistemologies does not exhaust the space of epistemic possibilities. This observation weakens van Fraassen's case for voluntarist epistemology.

(c) van Fraassen has done too little to motivate *moderate* voluntarism; *radical* voluntarism remains a serious contender.

(d) van Fraassen's account of scientific revolutions does not give us an altogether compelling case for epistemic voluntarism. Still the account contains a wealth of intriguing ideas that are well worthy of further development, even outside the context of scientific revolutions.

(e) Boghossian's arguments against relativism do not threaten van Fraassen's position.

5 Relativism in the Sociology of Scientific Knowledge

Introduction

SSK has been at the center of relativism-debates in the philosophy of science since the 1980s. Let there be no false suspense: I have tried to defend SSK, and contribute to it, for three decades. This section will therefore be much less critical than the last. I shall offer a detailed account of some of the central relativistic aspects of SSK, especially as these are found in the writings of Barry Barnes and David Bloor. Subsequently, I shall defend SSK against some recent criticisms coming from Paul Boghossian and Michael Friedman. I shall conclude by comparing the relativism of SSK with the relativism of Bas van Fraassen.

The Central Elements of SSK

I find it useful to distinguish among six core elements of SSK: the "Strong Program," the "Hesse-net," the "rule-following considerations," empiricism, the distinction between two strata of rationality, and the significance of fundamental scientific disagreements.

The Strong Program

The methodological "heart" of SSK is the following four tenets, first formulated by Bloor in 1976:

(1) [The Program of SSK] would be causal, that is, concerned with the conditions that bring about belief or states of knowledge. Naturally, there will be other types of causes apart from social ones that will cooperate in bringing about belief.

(2) It would be impartial with respect to truth and falsity, rationality or irrationality, success or failure. Both sides of these dichotomies will require explanation.

(3) It would be symmetrical in its style of explanation. The same types of cause would explain, say, true and false beliefs.

(4) It would be reflexive. In principle, its patterns of explanation would have to be applicable to sociology itself.[187]

Bloor calls this the "strong" – rather than the "weak" – program in SSK, first, because it is meant to apply to *all* sciences (including the humanities) and, second, because it calls for sociological explanations of both *true and false* beliefs.

The first three tenets are clearly in evidence in one of the early classics of SSK, Steven Shapin's "Homo Phrenologicus."[188] Shapin aims to do for scientific knowledge what anthropologists have done for cosmologies of preliterate cultures: to understand how *social order* relates to *natural order*. In this context, anthropologists speak of three kinds of social interests:

– an interest in protecting the community by predicting and explaining natural phenomena;

– an interest in making sense of, and coping with, one's position in the world; and

– an interest in maintaining or changing social hierarchies and division of labor.

Shapin seeks to identify these interests in the version of phrenology that was prevalent in Edinburgh roughly between 1800 and 1830.

---

[187] Bloor, *Knowledge*, p. 7.   [188] Shapin, "Homo Phrenologicus."

The basic assumptions of phrenological theory are, of course, well known: the mind is made up of around thirty "faculties"; each faculty is tied to a specific brain "organ"; the size of a brain-organ correlates with the degree to which one possesses the corresponding faculty; and the dimensions of the various brain-organs result in "bumps" in specific locations of the skull. The phrenologist is therefore able to predict talents and dispositions by inspecting people's heads.

Phrenologists took a deep interest in the human brain, producing maps of the cortex that are highly detailed and sophisticated. In other words, their interest in understanding natural phenomena cannot reasonably be doubted. In order to pinpoint the role of the other two kinds of interests, it is important to remember that the Edinburgh phrenologists came from the bourgeoisie, and that the period witnessed the introduction of a capitalist-industrial economy. The bourgeoisie used phrenology to make sense of, and to defend, this fundamental social-political change. Sometimes phrenologists invoked the large number of faculties in order to defend the increase in professional specialization and division of labor. (Traditional philosophy only knew of six such faculties.) On other occasions, phrenologists referred to a particular faculty – "conscientiousness" – to legitimate competition. Conscientiousness was the ability to work out one's social standing relative to others. And finally, phrenology also – at least metaphorically – illuminated the collapse of traditional hierarchies: mind was no longer above body; mind was dependent upon the body. This very opposition had in the past been used to highlight the difference between the "spirit" of the aristocracy and the "hand" of the servants and peasants.

Although Shapin does not refer in detail to Bloor's strong program, the first three tenets are easy to identify: his study is:

– *causal*, insofar as he seeks to identify some of the causes that made it natural for members of the bourgeoisie to reach for phrenological ideas;
– *impartial*, in that he does not take sides in the disputes between phrenologists and the older school-philosophy; and
– *symmetrical*, insofar as he explains the phrenologists' true and false beliefs about mind and brain in terms of the same general interests.

Hesse-Nets

Turning from methodology to substantive philosophical resources, Mary Hesse's work on the "network-model" of natural knowledge is arguably the main SSK "loan" from philosophy of science.[189]

---

[189] Barnes, "Conventional Character"; Bloor, "Durkheim and Mauss"; Hesse, *Structure*. I discuss this text in relation to scientific realism in Kusch, "Social Epistemology."

The natural starting point is the practice of attaching labels to phenomena picked out by social conventions. When speakers go beyond their original learning set for specific labels, they do so on the basis of similarity judgements between exemplars of the set and newly encountered features of their environment. As we shall see later – when talking about "finitism" – such similarity judgements are of great interest to the sociologist (not least when trying to understand the roles of models and analogues in the science).[190]

Similarity judgements are of special interest for the sociologist, since they are always in principle contestable. Different speakers judge similarities in different ways. Linguistic communities must therefore find ways of overruling and harmonizing individual speakers' similarity spaces. The social must ultimately trump the individual-psychological, albeit the existence of the former depends upon the existence of the latter.[191] Connecting the uses of different labels with simple laws – such as "water is wet" – is a crucial method for governing individual dispositions and inclinations regarding naming. These laws are agreed upon, and then taught and maintained, by teachers and other authorities. To use Émile Durkheim's signature term, these laws are thus "collective representations." Bloor highlights three facets of such representations: they allow speakers to competently use terms in new circumstances; they can be illuminating even when they do not underwrite successful technologies; and they typically are tied together in "networks."[192]

The problem of similarity judgements reappears when networks of laws are developed in light of novel phenomena. For instance, our ancestors needed to decide whether to group whales with mammals or with fish. The decision to prioritize the criterion of "suckling the young" over the criterion of "living in water" could not be made on the basis of perception alone. It required the interplay of sense-perception and the network of laws. Moreover, past decisions can later be reconsidered. Negotiation can always be resumed in light of new considerations.[193] Still, perceptual evidence almost always plays a crucial role. Hesse seeks to emphasize this role by speaking of a "correspondence postulate" guiding network engineering. Bloor prefers the term "adaptation postulate" in order to distance the account from the correspondence theory of truth and to signal Darwinian sympathies. It also serves to underline the thought that there is no one uniquely correct way of responding to an "indefinitely complex" reality.[194]

In addition to the "correspondence postulate," Hesse also introduces a second factor responsible for the relative stability of networks of laws: "coherence

---

[190] Bloor, "Durkheim and Mauss," 270.   [191] Ibid., 271.   [192] Ibid., 272–3.   [193] Ibid., 274.
[194] Ibid., 278.

conditions." These conditions are primarily "metaphysical principles" regulating and shaping a network as a whole. Typically, principles are expressed in preferences for certain metaphors or models, or else in specific strictly policed conceptual boundaries. The speakers take these principles to be obviously true or self-evident. But the self-evidence of a given principle is the effect of this principle's being treated as sacrosanct; it is not the cause. Bloor aims to connect Hesse's "metaphysical principles" to the anthropological concerns mentioned earlier in the context of Shapin's study of Edinburgh phrenologists. That is to say, he proposes that metaphysical principles play a central role in maintaining or challenging social order. We use our ideas about natural order in order to legitimize our preferred division of labor and hierarchies.[195]

Overall, Bloor suggests that Hesse's network supports the SSK hypothesis that knowledge is the resultant of two vectors: perceptual experience and social factors or dimensions such as social interests.[196] Elsewhere, Bloor and Barnes submit that Hesse's work also vindicates three further ideas: that "all cultures are equally near to nature" in that they "engage with nature according to the same general principles";[197] that there is "no place for the myth, much beloved by many realists, that science progresses by converging on the truth";[198] and that the predictive success of a theory is always the predictive success of the theory *as a whole*.[199]

The Rule-Following Considerations

Ludwig Wittgenstein's rule-following considerations ("RFC") are a further crucial philosophical resource for SSK. This is a difficult issue.[200] Here I can do no more than gesture at what is the central significance of the RFC for SSK.

There are four possible positions concerning rule-following and meaning. *Individualist meaning-determinism* holds that we can make sense of these phenomena on the level of a socially isolated individual, her mental and physical states, and especially her dispositions to act (e.g. to use signs) in appropriate ways. *Communitarian meaning-determinism* replaces the socially isolated individual with a social group. But it keeps the thought that meaning is to do with mental and physical dispositions to act.

Individualist meaning-finitism modifies the second component of individualist meaning-determinism. For the meaning-finitist, we learn rules or words by being taught a finite number of exemplars for acting. We apply our lesson in new

---

[195] Ibid., 283.   [196] Cf. Bloor, *Knowledge*, p. 32.
[197] Bloor, "Anti-Latour," 88; cf. Barnes, "Conventional Character," 316.
[198] Barnes, "Realism, Relativism," 143.   [199] Bloor, "Anti-Latour," 94.
[200] Bloor, *Wittgenstein*; Bloor, *Rules and Institutions*; Kusch, *Sceptical Guide*.

situations by assessing the similarity between the novel phenomena and the elements of our learning set. The application in question is thus based on analogical reasoning. Finally, *communitarian meaning-finitism* highlights the fact that similarities and analogies are always in principle contestable and that it needs the consensus of a relevant community to be counted as – to have the status of – someone who is competent in acting.

SSK is a form of communitarian meaning-finitism. This form of finitism is a kind of *semantic relativism*: different individuals or social groups might disagree on what constitutes following a rule or applying a term correctly, and there is no "God's-eye view" from which one of these positions is absolutely more true or more correct than another.

This importance of finitism for SSK goes beyond the domain of meaning. It applies also to action and scientific practice: scientific practice is not guided or determined by rules; it is based on precedents, analogies, and negotiation.

Empiricism

For Bloor, empiricism is primarily "a [causal] psychological learning theory."[201] The emphasis on empiricism as a *scientific* theory stems from Bloor's desire to sharply separate SSK from philosophy. For instance, Bloor writes that "to ask questions of the sort which philosophers address to themselves is usually to paralyze the mind," and elsewhere he presents SSK as the successor to philosophy.[202] Bloor admires empirical science since "[i]n the main, [it] is causal, theoretical, value-neutral, often reductionist, to an extent empiricist, and ultimately materialistic."[203] Barnes advocates empiricism as a policy when he asks SSK-scholars to honor the "empiricist stereotype" to "valorize the particular and engender skepticism about . . . universal claims."[204]

Bloor and Barnes emphasize that their empiricism is relativistic. Barnes notes that "rationalists frequently point out that empiricism implies relativism, which is of course perfectly correct."[205] This remark follows on from the previously cited claim that empiricism valorizes attention to the local and is skeptical of generalizations. Barnes's thought fits with the general SSK-relativist principle that all beliefs "must be accounted for by finding the specific, local causes of [their] credibility":[206]

> For the [SSK-] relativist there is no sense attached to the idea that some standards or beliefs are really rational as distinct from merely locally

---

[201] Bloor, *Knowledge*, pp. 31, 34.   [202] Bloor, *Wittgenstein*, p. 182; Bloor, *Knowledge,* p. 52.
[203] Bloor, *Knowledge*, p. 157.   [204] Barnes, "Acceptance," 378.   [205] Ibid., 381.
[206] Barnes and Bloor, "Relativism," 23.

accepted as such. ... [He] thinks that there are no context-free or super-cultural norms of rationality.[207]

Bloor expresses admiration for the logical empiricist Philipp Frank, who in *Wahrheit: Relativ oder Absolut?* claims that the progress of science amounts to "an increase in 'relativisation.' Ever more concepts are modified with the expression 'relative to a given frame of reference'."[208] Bloor takes Frank to confirm relativism as an empirical hypothesis about science.

Rationality

In developing a theory of rationality, SSK – like van Fraassen – draws on the empiricist tradition. But, whereas van Fraassen invokes the "radical empiricist" William James, Bloor is indebted to the empiricist *psychologism* of David Hume and John Stuart Mill. For instance, Bloor reconstructs Frege's criticism of Mill's psychologism in an effort to motivate the sociology of knowledge. As Bloor has it, Frege was right at least to the extent that Mill's psychological-inductive analysis of arithmetic does not (on its own) deliver the right kind of objectivity. But that does not mean that Bloor accepts Frege's Platonism. Instead, Bloor suggests that the required objectivity is to be found in a combination of individual psychology and social institutions.[209] And else-where, Bloor claims that Nuel Belnap's four rules meant to capture "our ... notion of deducibility" are indeed "expressions of 'thinking habits'."[210] One such rule is "Weakening" (" $\vdash$ " stands for deducibility):

From $p, \ldots, p_n \vdash r$ one can infer $p, \ldots, p_n, q \vdash r$

This corresponds to the assumption in psychological learning theory that irrelevant information does not disrupt well-reinforced habits. Bloor writes: "When psychologists build their learning-theories they tend to assume that organisms have brains that obey rules rather like these."[211] Bloor also reads Carnap's lambda-parameter through his sociological concerns: "Carnap had located a sociological variable at the heart of his formal analysis. ... why does the social group have this rather than that inductive strategy?"[212] The interplay of psychological and sociological concerns is furthermore visible where Bloor, in his analysis of the conflict between traditional logic and relevance logic, distinguishes between three interacting elements: deductive intuitions, studied by the psychologist; interests and needs of a relevant

---

[207] Ibid., p. 27.   [208] Frank, *Wahrheit*, p. 73.   [209] Bloor, *Knowledge*, pp. 92–96.
[210] Bloor, *Wittgenstein*, p. 116. Cf. Wittgenstein, *Remarks*, I, 131.
[211] Bloor, *Wittgenstein*, p. 116.   [212] Bloor, "Relativism," 449.

community, studied by sociologists; and "language-games" of logic and mathematics.[213]

Finally, on a more general level, the psychological and the sociological dimensions are first distinguished by Barnes in 1976. He distinguishes between two kinds of rationality: "natural" and "normative" (evaluative, prescriptive) rationality. "Natural rationality" is a "psychological concept" and covers "natural reasoning proclivities and capacities ... discernible in the thinking of all cultures."[214] Normative rationality qua sociological concept covers "how [a] culture, or some part of it, thinks inference ought to proceed." It is "a set of norms or conventions."[215] Barnes insists that there should be "no opposition between causality and rationality" as far as natural or normative rationality is concerned.[216]

Fundamental Scientific Disagreements

SSK seeks to respond to Kuhn. It rejects Kuhn's account of normal science and revolutions. Barnes complains that often Kuhn "creates the impression" that "normal scientists are [. . .] rational automata" following methodological rules.[217] Kuhn invites the thought that *finitism* only applies to revolutionary, but not to normal, science. Barnes claims that the historical record proves otherwise: "any particular change which occurs in a revolutionary episode can occur equally in a period of normal science, whether it be meaning change, technical change, the inventions of new problem-solutions, or the emergence of new standards of judgements."[218] Once this is recognized, Barnes claims, we have every reason to reject Kuhn's "functionalist" account of revolutions: "Hence there is nothing to compel a leap out of the system [that is, out of the old paradigm]: nothing makes it necessary to replace, rather than to develop, existing practice."[219]

The second part of the SSK response to Kuhn – a finitist rendering of language, paradigms, theories, and values – is much more positive. Consider language first. Take a child learning the words "duck" and "swan" from an adult who points out clear examples of each category. The child thereby learns, Barnes says, two "communally sanctioned similarity relations."[220] The same applies to scientific language: "the use of the concepts of physics must be learnt via accepted problem-solutions or paradigms."[221] Here, too, communally sanctioned similarity relations are key. The finitist thought also applies to scientific work and theories.

---

[213] Bloor, *Wittgenstein*, chapters 6 and 7.   [214] Barnes, "Natural Rationality," 115–16, 120.
[215] Ibid., 117.   [216] Bloor, "Epistemology," 393.   [217] Barnes, *Kuhn*, pp. 83–4.
[218] Ibid., p. 86.   [219] Ibid.   [220] Ibid., p. 24.   [221] Ibid., p. 35.

Paradigms are exemplary problem-solutions, models, to which new situations are (to be) assimilated.[222] And a theory is a "cluster of accepted problem-solutions" resembling each other. Such resemblances are expressed in constants or formal laws. But there is not, beyond the resemblances, a "basic logical structure, or form, or essence, 'within', 'behind' or 'above' any application of a theory."[223] Barnes sees finitism also as crucial for understanding values. Values are not rule-like: they are glosses on a "continuing, active, revisable clustering of particular instances."[224] This is why values cannot give the sort of guidance in revolutions that Kuhn in 1977 takes them to provide.

SSK goes beyond Kuhn in emphasizing what I shall call "socially attuned wide-scope scientific rationality." This is linked to SSK's crucial interest in fundamental scientific disagreements. Consider for instance Shapin's 1996 book on the Scientific Revolution[225] and especially on the controversies between Galileo and the Jesuits, between Copernicans and their enemies, between Hobbes and Boyle, or between Hooke and Newton. In each instance, Shapin makes the case that the historical actors had to rationally navigate socially pressing issues like:

- *Metaphysics*, e.g. Is everything in nature a machine?
- *Instruments*, e.g. What use is to be made of telescopes or microscopes?
- *Epistemology*, e.g. Can knowledge be certain? Who is a reliable testifier?
- *Governance*, e.g. How should natural philosophy be governed?
- *Theology*, e.g. What in natural philosophy endangers, what supports belief in God?
- *Disciplinary Hierarchies*, e.g. How does physics relate to biology? Astronomy to astrology?
- *Politics and Economics*, e.g. How can natural philosophy help maintain social peace or be economically useful?
- *Audience*, e.g. Whom should natural philosophy address? And in what language?
- *Scientific Identity*, e.g. Should the natural philosopher be a gentleman, a professor, a cleric, or a courtier?
- *Military*, e.g. What can natural philosophy offer ballistics?

The need to address these issues *together with* so-called "technical content" was especially prominent in cases when actors found themselves in situations where they were unable to agree on data, instruments, and theories – all at once.

---

[222] Ibid., p. 47.   [223] Ibid., p. 121.   [224] Ibid., p. 124.   [225] Shapin, *Scientific Revolution*.

SSK-theorists' focus on fundamental scientific disagreements is part and parcel of SSK-relativism. First, for SSK, the study of various forms of underdetermination is meant to establish the crucial role of socially attuned widescope rationality. Fundamental scientific disagreements are important because they bring out what is not always visible in more pedestrian scientific work, to wit, that justification is invariably a local, contingent, relative, finitist phenomenon.

Second, SSK takes its studies to show that fundamental scientific disagreements are not conflicts between reason and unreason but controversies between naturally rational actors. This is taken to support a form of psychologism: all normal scientific actors have precisely the kind of rationality that psychologists (rather than philosophers!) investigate. Third, since natural rationality is shared, fundamental scientific disagreements concern conflicts at the level of culture-specific normative rationalities. This is not to deny that competing scientists (or adherents to different paradigms) might overlap in their normative rationalities. Still, for SSK, this is not a reason to assume that there is an essential core to such rationalities. In other words, SSK commits to a sociologism as far as normative rationalities are concerned: normative rationalities vary with social context.

Fourth, if the preceding three ideas are accepted, SSK holds; then relativism can be said to be confirmed both as a research strategy (look for local and variable causes of credibility!) and as a causal hypothesis: scientific beliefs can be fully accounted for by local and variable causes of credibility; there is no good scientific reason to postulate any rational absolutes. Fifth, and finally, how does SSK stand vis-à-vis the sciences it studies? The clearest answer is given when Bloor – tongue in cheek – speaks of SSK as "a Higher Criticism of Science."[226] That is to say, "SSK is just the extension of science to the study of itself."[227]

Intermediate Summary

SSK clearly falls within the relativist spectrum of Section 2. To begin with, SSK is clearly committed to *methodological* relativism: the impartiality and symmetry tenets of the Strong Program ask the sociologists to treat the beliefs of all groups impartially *as on a par* and to explain all scientific beliefs in terms of the same general types of social causes. Moreover, as the reflexivity principle has it, there is no privileged position for the SSK-practitioners: their beliefs are to be explored in the same ways as those of others.

Turning from methodology to philosophical position, SSK-relativism embodies a particularist form of DEPENDENCE. Central aspects of knowledge

---

[226] Briatte, "Interview."   [227] Shapin, "Here and Everywhere," 292.

and belief are relative to human psychology and to the local normative rationality of particular groups or cultures. Responses to new features of experience are guided by culturally sanctioned exemplars, social interests, and negotiation. PLURALITY is also an obvious commitment. There is always a plurality of possible ways to develop a given (scientific) practice; always a plurality of typifications, models, responses to novelty, and ways of developing taxonomies. Moreover, SSK accepts CONFLICT: this goes with the central position accorded to studies of fundamental disagreements. Such disagreements might – but need not – involve forms of methodological and semantic incommensurability. Since SSK is skeptical of the distinction between "normal" and "revolutionary" phases of science, it does not accept a Kuhnian conception of CONVERSION. Still, SSK obviously does accept that changes in scientific culture are not compelled in terms of neutral and universal rational principles and evidence on their own. Fundamental changes in science may well concern received patterns of reasoning.

Finally, with respect to SYMMETRY, the claim that "all cultures are equidistant from nature" may easily strike one as an acceptance of EQUAL VALIDITY. But that would be a misunderstanding. After all, the equidistance is explained by saying that all cultures rely on the same general principles for engaging with nature. And these "general principles" were the elements of the Hesse-net. But, while EQUAL VALIDITY is not a substantive element of SSK-relativism, two other subcategories of SYMMETRY are undoubtedly present: LOCALITY and NONNEUTRALITY.

Answering Boghossian

SSK has been criticized and attacked for almost five decades. I cannot review and answer all these criticisms here.[228] I shall focus on the influential arguments Boghossian advances against epistemic relativism in general. My aim is to show that SSK has the resources to rebut these arguments.

The natural starting point is the relationship between relativism and absolutism.[229] Bloor and Boghossian agree that to be a relativist is to deny absolutism and that to be an absolutist is to deny relativism. *Tertium non datur.* Bloor writes: "relativism is the negation of absolutism. To be a relativist is to deny that there is such a thing as absolute knowledge and absolute truth." Bloor even makes explicit what he means when he speaks of "absolute knowledge": it would be "perfect, unchanging, and unqualified by limitations of time, space,

---

[228] See e.g. Bloor, "Relativism."

[229] I here develop further a line of argument first presented in Kusch, "Relativism in the Sociology of Scientific Knowledge," 197–8.

and perspective. It would not be conjectural, hypothetical, or approximate, or depend on the circumstances of the knowing subject."[230]

Despite the consensus on the *tertium non datur*, Boghossian and SSK differ on what is the best argument in defense of nonabsolutism. As we saw earlier, Boghossian's relativist builds her case on the illegitimacy of circular justification. Barnes and Bloor are aware of the issue, as the following passage shows:

> In the last analysis, he [the SSK-relativist] will acknowledge that his justifications will stop at some principle or alleged matter of fact that only has local credibility. The only alternative is that justifications will begin to run in a circle and assume what they were meant to justify.[231]

Barnes and Bloor insist here that the position of the SSK-relativist does not have an absolute or ultimate foundation. The choice, therefore, can only be between a *circular justification* and a *justification breaking off* at a local and contingent point. Given the two options, Barnes and Bloor prefer acknowledging the inevitability of the contingent stopping point. This is, of course, the relativist tenet of LOCALITY.

The important difference from Boghossian's relativist is that Barnes and Bloor do not invoke rule-circularity in order to deny the very possibility of justifying our epistemic principles or networks of laws. They invoke circularity in order to make the case for a different understanding of justification, an understanding that lets justifications come to an end with "some principle or alleged matter of fact that only has local credibility." This position clearly is similar, and perhaps indebted, to the well-known §217 of Ludwig Wittgenstein's *Philosophical Investigations*: "If I have exhausted the justifications, I have reached bedrock and my spade is turned. Then I am inclined to say: 'This is simply what I do.'" It also resonates with Karl Popper's (relativistic[232]) thought that the stopping points for the justification of our observational statements are contingent.[233]

Bloor has also replied directly to Boghossian's critique of the relativist argument against absolutism. Recall that Boghossian believes he can block the argument by insisting that we are entitled to use our very epistemic principles in order to justify these principles. At least, we are so entitled as long as these principles have not become independently doubtful. Bloor is skeptical that this move can help the absolutist: "if absolutists can use circular arguments to justify their position, then relativists can also avail themselves of this move."[234]

---

[230] Bloor, "Relativism," 436–7.

[231] Barnes and Bloor, "Relativism," 27; Seidel, "Epistemic Relativist," 135.

[232] Newton-Smith, *Rationality of Science*, pp. 59–64.   [233] Popper, *Scientific Discovery*, Ch. 5.

[234] Bloor, "Epistemic Grace," 261.

In other words, even if we accept epistemic circularity, this does not automatically allow us to draw the conclusion that our epistemic system is better than another *in any absolute sense of the term*.

Up to this point, I have explained how SSK-relativism relates to Boghossian's arguments for and against nonabsolutism. It is also worth repeating how SSK itself aims to make the case against absolutism. First and foremost, there is the detailed historical and sociological work on fundamental scientific disagreements canvassed earlier. This work is taken to support the "historicist" generalization that justification is invariably local, contingent, and relative. Here, SSK-theorists are not worried that the work suggesting this relativist generalization is itself based upon a relativist methodology (i.e. the tenets of the "Strong Program"). No doubt Barnes and Bloor would regard this circularity as inevitable and beneficial rather than avoidable or vicious. Moreover, SSK's historical scholarship is also assumed to display shared psychological reasoning propensities – propensities that owe their existence to the contingencies of our evolutionary history. I called this element "psychologistic" earlier. SSK "historicism" and "psychologism" are part and parcel of SSK's naturalism, the thought that we cannot ever "transcend the machinery of our brains and the deliverances of our sense organs, the culture we occupy and the traditions on which we depend."[235]

To sum up, SSK-relativism is not obviously threatened by Boghossian's way of dismissing arguments against absolutism.

Turning to Boghossian's critical reflections on PLURALITY, remember that he poses a dilemma for the relativist concerning Bellarmine's principle of *Revelation*. Assume – first horn – that the relativist believes *Revelation* to be *fundamental* in Bellarmine's "epistemic system" of epistemic principles. In doing so, the relativist assumes herself to be dealing with a "genuine alternative" to our epistemic system (since, presumably, "we" do not accept *Revelation*). Recall here that the relativist tenet of PLURALITY needs there to be a number of genuine alternatives. The further thought is that, as underived elements, fundamental principles cannot be criticized on the ground that they fail to follow from other principles. Boghossian is, of course, unconvinced. He counters by arguing that, if *Revelation* is fundamental for Bellarmine, then the cardinal acts in an epistemically arbitrary – and hence irrational – way: concerning clouds and phases of the moon, he relies on *Observation*; concerning the issue of Copernicanism, he leans on *Revelation*. To be consistent, Bellarmine should act in accordance with one and the same principle for one and the same subject matter.

---

[235] Bloor, "Epistemic Grace," 252.

Let us turn to the second horn. Let the relativist reply by saying that Bellarmine did in fact have good reasons for using *Revelation* for some but not all phenomena of the heavens. One reason might be the distinction between the "sublunar" and "celestial" realms. Most astronomers and physicists at the time agreed that the two realms were governed by different laws of nature. It thus was not irrational to believe that they therefore called for the operation of different epistemic principles: *Observation* for the sublunar and *Revelation* for the celestial. Alternatively, Bellarmine might have distinguished the proper fields of application of the two principles in terms of the observable/unobservable opposition: *Observation* for the former and *Revelation* for the latter.[236] Again, Boghossian finds this solution unsatisfactory (though he does not go into any detail). His thought seems to be that if there is a principle regulating the proper use of *Revelation*, then *Revelation* is no longer fundamental. And if *Revelation* is not fundamental, then we can empirically test the assumptions it involves; for example, that the Bible was dictated by the "Holy Spirit."[237]

I am not persuaded. I agree with the second-horn option that Bellarmine had criteria governing when *Revelation* trumps *Observation* and when it does not. But I do not accept that this in itself reduces *Revelation* to being derived rather than fundamental. Remember Boghossian's formulation of *Observation*:

> (*Observation*) For any observational proposition p, if it visually seems to S that p and circumstantial conditions D obtain, then S is prima facie justified in believing p.[238]

Boghossian takes it for granted that this principle *is* fundamental for us. And yet, here too, we obviously have further criteria governing when and where observation is to be used and when it is to give way to other epistemic resources, like testimony or reasoning. Surely Boghossian accepts as much. But if he does, then his reflections about the second horn are mistaken. If *Observation* is a fundamental principle *despite* being governed in its application by further principles, then *Revelation* can be a fundamental principle, too. The fact that Bellarmine accepts *Revelation* does not commit him to applying this principle without restrictions. Boghossian tells us that by "fundamental principle" he means "a principle whose correctness cannot be derived from the correctness of other epistemic principles."[239] Given this definition, *Revelation* can still be fundamental; after all, it is not that we "derive" *Revelation* from criteria governing its application.

There is a further problem, too, with Boghossian's thinking about epistemic principles. He notes that

---

[236] There is good evidence that Bellarmine did just that. Cf. Bellarmine, "Letter."
[237] Boghossian, *Fear*, pp. 104–5.   [238] Ibid., p. 64   [239] Ibid., p. 67.

> it is hard to say, even as a purely descriptive matter, precisely which epistemic principles we operate with ... [and that] ... the idea is not that we *grasp* Observation explicitly ... rather, the idea is that we *operate according to* Observation: it is *implicit* in our practice, rather than explicit in our formulations.[240]

It is true, of course, that *Observation* does not feature in the everyday or scientific discourses of epistemic "actors"; it is only epistemological "analysts" who seek to formulate it explicitly. At the same time, it is worth remembering that many other – more or less fundamental – epistemic principles do in fact regularly appear explicitly even in actors' discourse. After all, scientists often formulate methodological rules and policies in order to defend their results, attack the results of others, or simply teach the next generation. SSK and Kuhn take it that such formulations are secondary with respect to exemplars and that the correct application of a rule depends upon the local, natural, and social circumstances of the respective users. (This is the basic idea of communitarian finitism and as clear an expression of LOCALITY as any.)

Does Boghossian succeed in sidestepping these relativistic considerations by treating epistemic principles not as actors' guides to action but as analysts' ways of capturing and summarizing dispositions to act and judge in epistemically relevant ways? I think not. To begin with, SSK accepts that formulations of epistemic principles are often analysts' hypotheses meant to capture some of the actors' dispositions and practices. But SSK is unlikely to go along with Boghossian's implicit assumption that there is one unique set of epistemic axioms that best fulfils this role. SSK recognizes the under-determination of epistemological hypotheses by the actors' observed behavior.

The case of logic is directly parallel: there is more than one logical system claiming to capture our logical dispositions or intuitions; and the different systems each come with their specific costs and benefits. None does justice to all the data, and – if logical "pluralists" are to be believed – we may well be stuck with an irreducible *plurality* of logics.[241] Why should the case be different for epistemology? One does not need to be a relativist to recognize that here too there are numerous competing ways of rendering our epistemic folkways, and there may well not be *the one and only* correct way.[242] If that is true, then *Revelation* may be *fundamental* for Bellarmine according to one epistemologist's rendering and *derived* according to another epistemologist's

---

[240] Ibid., p. 65.   [241] Cf. Beall and Restall, *Logical Pluralism*.
[242] Cf. e.g. Alston, "Epistemic Desiderata."

reconstruction. This scenario introduces an instability that seems to damage Boghossian's absolutism more than SSK-relativism.

Finally, Barnes and Bloor would also be uncomfortable with Boghossian's "foundationalist" idiom of fundamental and derived principles. Hesse-networks and finitism suggest a *coherentist* rather than a foundationalist imagery, and a focus on exemplary particulars rather than rule-like entities. This perspective also makes it harder to distinguish neatly between epistemic and nonepistemic elements. This is, of course, clear enough in the case of Bellarmine, for whom epistemic, metaphysical, theological, ethical, and political considerations were so tightly intertwined that to discuss any one of them in isolation is not a helpful idealization but a gross distortion.[243] To sum up, we might say that whereas Boghossian's reflections on epistemology are "isolationist" and "foundational-ist," SSK's rendering is "holist" and "coherentist."

I can be brief about Boghossian's remaining four anti-relativist consider-ations. Does SSK-relativism refute itself? I do not think so. Since SSK is not committed to EQUAL VALIDITY, it is not precluded from criticizing absolutist viewpoints. And the absolutist who so tailors their principles that relativism turns out to be wrong deviates radically from the way epistemology functions in most of our philosophical traditions.

Is the SSK-relativist guilty of "double-think"? Is her relativist theory com-patible with being fully committed to particular beliefs, practices, or standards? When the SSK-relativist engages in a case study – say a historical study of Bellarmine's belief system – then she suspends judgement concerning the truth and justifiability of Bellarmine's beliefs. And yet, outside the study, she remains fully committed to, say, Copernicanism and possibly atheism. Is that a problem? I cannot see why it should be. Surely, we all are able to compartmentalize our intellectual activity, and in different "compartments" we work with different commitments.

Moreover, I do not think that SSK holds a problematic version of "absolutist relativism." It is true that SSK does not treat all rationality as of one kind. There is natural rationality, studied by psychologists, and there is normative rational-ity, studied by the sociologist and historian. It is also true that natural rationality is shared by almost all humans. But that it is so shared does not raise it to the level of being absolute in any heavyweight sense of the term. It is the product of our contingent evolutionary history, and it can be overruled for purposes of science or art.

---

[243] Cf. Biagioli, *Galileo, Courtier*; Blackwell, *Galileo, Bellarmine*; Finocchiaro, *Retrying Galileo*; Heilbron, *Galileo*.

Finally, SSK-relativism is not threatened by the proposal that whatever relativity there is in our epistemic practices can be accounted for in terms of the vagueness of our absolute principles. SSK would answer here very much as I suggested earlier the voluntarist might reply: we should not expect this methodology to lead to one unique outcome. And, at least for the purposes of sociology and history, we should not ignore the actors' own perspectives on their epistemic folkways.

SSK and Voluntarist-Constructive Empiricism

I regard voluntarist-constructive empiricism (= "VCE") and SSK as the most promising forms of relativism in the contemporary study of science. In this section, I shall explore some of their commonalities and differences.

Empiricism

Empiricism seems a natural breeding ground and resource for relativist positions. VCE and SSK are equally telling and clear on this issue. Of course, not every empiricist is a relativist; and not every relativist is an empiricist. Still, there surely is a book to be written about the historical links between empiricism and relativism.

VCE and SSK differ in their understanding of empiricism. VCE redefines empiricism as a stance, and aims to learn from James's "radical empiricism." SSK instead is eager to capture the empiricism in the sciences themselves, and insists that empiricism is at heart a psychological learning theory. Earlier, I suggested that this rendering is connected to Bloor's desire to sharply separate SSK from philosophy. This is one of the (few) points where Bloor and I differ. I cannot square his dismissive anti-philosophical attitude with his extensive and productive use of – amongst others – Anscombe, Carnap, Hesse, Hume, Kripke, Kuhn, and Wittgenstein. There must be something valuable about philosophy if these thinkers can prove so useful for SSK. And it is not just valuable for SSK: many scientists greatly value philosophical input. van Fraassen's strong standing amongst quantum physicists is an obvious case in point.[244]

SSK-theorists have not discussed *constructive empiricism*. There are both commonalities and differences. To begin with, SSK-theorists tend to sound like scientific realists about the *social* sciences. Barnes and Bloor are not shying away from positing theoretical-unobservable entities like classes, interests, or social structures. When it comes to *basic* categories of social life, SSK-theorists do not foreground their anti-realist view that reality has no one fixed structure or

---

[244] van Fraassen, *Quantum Mechanics*.

that it allows numerous alternative conceptualizations. Nor do SSK-theorists deny that their historical case studies can be, and often are, true to the historical facts. I suspect Barnes and Bloor would agree with Harry Collins, who writes: "I endorse realism as an attitude both for scientists at their work and for sociologists at theirs."[245] There is no suggestion in the context of this endorsement that would limit the realism to observables.

Other passages point in a different direction. Barnes insists that his interpretation of Hesse's network is "uncompromisingly 'instrumentalist'"[246] and Bloor attacks the "naïve" assumption of a "one-to-one link" between terms of a predictively successful theory and natural kinds in the world. ("If the talk is about electrons or microbes, then there must be electrons or microbes."[247]) In another place, Bloor comes close to formulating the "pessimistic meta-induction" by insisting that all scientific theories eventually face competitors or alternatives with different theoretical terms.[248] Still, Bloor does not urge us to suspend judgement with respect to our current theories – or at least their theoretical entities.

Perhaps SSK's position could be strengthened by invoking an idea from *Image*: to wit, the claim that "immersion in the theoretical world-picture does not preclude 'bracketing' its ontological implications."[249] SSK would then be saying that natural and social scientists are immersed in a realist idiom that is highly productive and crucial for their work. But SSK-analysts are able and entitled to "bracket" some of these ontological implications. Taken in this way, SSK and VCE can be friends.

In the vicinity of their shared empiricism lie other ideas on which VCE and SSK converge: a constructivist take on models and representations; the stress on circularity in the study of science (we need science to understand science); and anthropocentrism: that is, the thought that there is no escaping our limited perspectives, as these have been shaped by evolution. All these are anti-absolutist, empiricist, and thus relativist themes.

Stances, Impulses, Interests

In explaining important features of science, VCE and SSK both look beyond belief or doctrine. In VCE, the terms "stance" and "impulse" are central. I agree that stances are important in science and philosophy, and I see merit in interpreting relativism itself as a stance. That said, I suspect Barnes and Bloor would not be fully satisfied with the theory of stances as it stands: from a sociological

---

[245] Collins, *Gravity's Shadow*, p. 15.   [246] Barnes, "Conventional Character," 307.

[247] Bloor, "Anti-Latour," 94.   [248] Ibid., 106.

[249] van Fraassen, *Scientific Image*, loc. 41,072.

point of view, van Fraassen says too little about how stances relate to social institutions or social order more generally.

Moreover, from the perspective of SSK, van Fraassen's explanation of how a new paradigm becomes a "live option" suffers from a similar shortcoming. van Fraassen suggests that it needs "emotion," "despair," or similar "impulses" to bring about such a change. Here, too, SSK would urge VCE to do greater justice to social dimensions, say by relating emotions to "interests." "Interest" is one key exemplar for SSK precisely because, starting with the Marxist tradition, it has been taken in a social or sociological vein. Interests are shared.

Wittgenstein

While Wittgenstein is front and center in SSK, he rarely appears in van Fraassen's oeuvre. Still, as I proposed earlier, *Representation* outlines what one might call a "Wittgensteinian Kantianism" of sorts. Central in this perspective is the priority of pragmatics over semantics, the thought of the "essential indexical" and locally varying interpretations of rules and concepts. This jibes well with SSK-finitism. But some differences remain. When discussing van Fraassen's take on "*sola experientia!*" earlier, I noted that he assumes far greater semantic stability than Feyerabend does. I suspect that SSK-theorists would side with Feyerabend. A similar disagreement is to be expected concerning van Fraassen's thought that scientific progress involves the discovery of ambiguities in scientific language. From a meaning-finitist perspective, this seems a problematic claim. Linguistic ambiguities are in the eye of the beholder: they do not have an existence independently of the judgements of competent speakers. Ambiguities are *constructed, not discovered*.

Rationality

Both SSK and VCE develop *stratified* conceptions of rationality. In the case of VCE, the two layers are general principles of rationality (logic, theory of probability), on the one hand, and the normative commitments resulting from stances, on the other. In SSK, the two strata are the natural rationality identified by psychologists and the normative-cultural rationality studied by the social sciences. In the case of SSK, the perspective on rationality is descriptive-explanatory; in the case of VCE, it is normative-evaluative (based on the intuition of "no-self-sabotage"). Moreover, unlike Priest, van Fraassen favors moderate over radical voluntarism: that is, he insists on a sharp dividing line between the two strata.

As far as the general lessons for relativism are at issue, it seems significant that both VCE and SSK opt for a bifurcation concerning rationality. This allows both of them to have something of a stable (though minimalist) backdrop of rationality, a backdrop against which differences can be accounted for. This backdrop would remain even if one opted for radical voluntarism, albeit it would reduce the scope of the lower stratum and make it more flexible.

The description–prescription opposition between the two accounts is stark, and no doubt Bloor would cite Wittgenstein against van Fraassen: "The danger here, I believe, is one of giving a justification of our procedure where there is no such thing as a justification and we ought simply to have said: that's how we do it."[250] Still, it seems to me that it is easy to overstate the differences in this area. Surely, when psychologists study basic rational skills of humans and animals, some normative perspective is unavoidable in order to tell apart rational from irrational dispositions. And a rough-and-ready criterion like "no-self-sabotage" seems as good a touchstone as any. Not to forget that there is an important commonality also in van Fraassen's and Bloor's positive attitude towards Carnap's "Principle of Tolerance." Undeniably, Bloor takes Carnap's talk of the choice of logical frameworks being "entirely free" much more seriously than van Fraassen does. The latter rules out, for instance, that Priest's "dialethism" is or could be "our" logic. I cannot imagine Bloor making a similar commitment.

Revolutions and the Role of Philosophy and Sociology of Knowledge

For VCE, scientific revolutions are of crucial significance: allegedly, VCE is the only theory that passes the test of "saving" their rationality. This is because, according to VCE, the lower stratum of rationality remains unchanged before, during, and after the revolution. The lower stratum is minimalist and leaves the choice of the upper, paradigm-relative rationality underdetermined. It is precisely this permissivism that leads to relativism. Anti-relativists like Friedman no doubt wonder how anyone could save rationality by capitulating to relativism.

SSK has no interest in proving that scientific revolutions are rational or progressive. Recall that Barnes is highly critical of the sociological "functionalism" of Kuhn's account of revolutions. From the perspective of SSK, van Fraassen is too close to Kuhn in this regard. Consider, for instance, how van Fraassen replies to Ernest McMullin's objection that in Galileo's writings one does not find anywhere the "despair" van Fraassen deems a defining feature of scientific revolutions. van Fraassen answers: "I had never really stopped to ask myself whether Galileo ... had suffered the sort of epistemic despair that I was describing. ... The absurdity was, it seems to me, a point of logic."[251]

---

[250] Wittgenstein, *Remarks*, II, 74; Bloor, *Wittgenstein*, p. 119.   [251] van Fraassen, "Replies," 3.

Undoubtedly, Barnes would object that this is a Kuhnian functionalist logic overriding historical evidence, and that the latter should give us reason to reject the former. SSK would respond similarly to van Fraassen's claims concerning objectifying and voluntarist epistemology. Whether, and to what extent, epistemology is intertwined with science cannot be decided from the philosophical armchair. This is something to be determined empirically: by observing and interviewing scientists or by wading through dusty old papers and books in archives and libraries.

van Fraassen has not, to date, engaged with SSK concerning the issue of what it means to take reflective responsibility for science. Friedman, however, has done so, and I shall use him as giving voice to a common disquiet about SSK amongst philosophers of science.[252] Friedman's first criticism is that SSK is philosophically naïve: it is blind to the fact that its own agenda is really philosophical: "Carnap plus Kuhn equals the philosophical agenda of SSK."[253] SSK is naïve or simplistic also in its understanding of Wittgenstein. As Friedman has it, Wittgenstein wanted to "show us how we can continue to take reflective responsibility for our most fundamental human practices" even while studying their basis and origin. Accordingly, there is "not a trace of socio-cultural relativism in Wittgenstein."[254] This is most obvious from the fact, Friedman alleges, that Wittgenstein concerned himself with the "'dignity' of logic and mathematics": "The mathematical proposition has the dignity of a rule."[255] Here, "dignity" is irreducibly evaluative-normative.

Friedman's second criticism is that SSK is ill-equipped for the task of "taking reflective responsibility" for science:

> One ... does not ... take responsibility by adopting the purely naturalistic and deliberatively non-evaluative point of view of the empirical ethnologist ... For the normativity of one's own standards is now explicitly reduced ... to the status of an otherwise arbitrary "preference" ... and the actual normative force of these standards is thereby inevitably dissolved.[256]

Is SSK really philosophically naïve? I am unconvinced. I cannot find that Barnes's and Bloor's intricate discussions of Kuhn, Hesse, Kripke, or Wittgenstein lack sophistication. Truth be told, I wonder whether it is not a little naïve to reduce SSK to "Carnap plus Kuhn." I hope the discussion of this section shows otherwise. As far as Wittgenstein is concerned, I am not

---

[252] Friedman, "Sociology of Scientific Knowledge."   [253] Ibid., 251.   [254] Ibid., 262–3.

[255] Ibid., 262; Wittgenstein, *Remarks*, I, 164.

[256] Friedman, "Sociology of Scientific Knowledge," 264.

persuaded that a quick reference to "the dignity of the rule" proves that Wittgenstein is in Friedman's camp. After all, Wittgenstein speaks also of the "dignity" of "the office of a king" and refers its study to anthropological analysis.[257]

Moreover, I struggle to accept Friedman's division of labor: causality for SSK, normativity (and thus reflective responsibility) for philosophy. First, although Bloor[258] scoffs at the idea of taking reflective responsibility, remember that he too wants SSK to be a "higher criticism of science." Put differently, one does take reflective responsibility when one identifies the local and contingent causes of the credibility of scientific beliefs. Second, SSK does not deny the importance of normative questions. But it insists that normative inquiry has to start from a detailed descriptive-explanatory account. Barnes praises Kuhn for doing just that.[259]

Third, Friedman is wrong to say that the ethnologist's perspective "dissolves" "normative force" and reduces standards "to the status of an ... arbitrary 'preference'." Something is *arbitrary* if it is "based on random choice or personal whim, rather than any reason or system."[260] Something is *contingent* if its existence depends on something else. The ethnologist's perspective is concerned with the dependence of beliefs on local causes of credibility, not searching for random choices or whim.

Fourth, Friedman is right in saying that SSK does not offer a general normative theory of scientific rationality. But SSK does not simply overlook this task; rather, it provides empirical arguments to the effect that the goal of such a theory is illusory. What normative theories there can be have to be built upon descriptive accounts of science, and they can only be local at best. Scientific reasoning is too complex, varied, and intertwined for us to be able to identify its unique form.

I conclude that van Fraassen has not convincingly discharged the task he sets himself: that is, to give a compelling account of scientific revolutions and to take reflective responsibility for science in the progress. His position is not strengthened by letting Friedman press the case against SSK.

Summary

The main results of this section can be summarized as follows.

(1) SSK is a form of methodological and philosophical-substantive (epistemic) relativism in the sense of Section 2.

---

[257] Wittgenstein, *Nachlass*, pp. 222–12.   [258] Bloor, *Enigma*, p. 494.
[259] Barnes, *Kuhn*, p. 60.   [260] *Lexico*, "Arbitrary."

(2) The methodological relativism centers on the "strong program." Shapin's case study of phrenology is a case in point.

(3) Hesse's network-model of natural knowledge and Wittgenstein's RFC are central pillars of SSK's philosophical-substantive relativism.

(4) SSK is also influenced by the tradition of psychologistic empiricism. This tradition informs the two-strata-view of rationality. "Natural rationality" is a psychological concept covering reasoning dispositions found in all cultures. "Normative rationality" is a sociological concept in that it refers to culture-specific conventions for reasoning.

(5) SSK rejects Kuhn's "functionalist" understanding of scientific revolutions and stresses the role of finitism in all phases of scientific work. SSK-studies of fundamental scientific disagreements are meant to highlight the importance of socially attuned wide-scope scientific rationality.

(6) SSK has satisfactory answers to the battery of arguments Boghossian directs at epistemic relativism.

(7) The contrast with Boghossian brings out clearly that SSK rejects isolationism (i.e. the thought that the epistemic realm can systematically be separated from other realms) and fundamentalism (i.e. the thought that the epistemic is neatly ordered into more or less fundamental principles).

(8) SSK and VCE share a historical debt to empiricism, and SSK is not far from constructive empiricism.

   (a) SSK's studies of the role of social interests are similar to VCE's insistence on the presence of stances and impulses. But SSK has much more to say about the role of social order and social change. The perspective of VCE is too individualistic.

   (b) Prima facie, it seems that SSK's and VCE's investigations into rationality are fundamentally different: the one focuses on causal-explanatory questions, the other on normative issues. Still, there is common ground here too: van Fraassen's core criterion of rationality – no-self-sabotage – must play an obvious role in psychological and biological studies of animal cognition.

   (c) As far as scientific revolutions are concerned, SSK raises serious doubts about the Kuhnian framework van Fraassen takes for granted.

   (d) van Fraassen's and Friedman's specific efforts to "take reflective responsibility" for science are in tension with the perspective of SSK. For SSK, such "taking responsibility" must focus on social-political dimensions of science; the goal of a normative theory of scientific rationality is a chimera.

6 Relativism and Post-Truth

Introduction

By now, I hope to have shown that both VCE and SSK are important and thought-provoking forms of relativism that have rich intellectual resources to block or deflect criticisms, on the one hand, and to illuminate numerous features of scientific work and rationality, on the other. I would be satisfied if this Element triggered additional charitable exploration of these and other relativistic proposals in the philosophy of science. At the same time, I am unsure whether such charitable exploration should realistically be expected any time soon. Lorraine Daston, the distinguished historian of science, recently observed that, in her field, relativism belongs with "all the other ghouls and goblins allegedly let loose" by Kuhn – that today "elicit barely a yawn."[261] Daston's assessment is also true, I fear, for most philosophers of science.

And yet, there are grounds for optimism, too. One particularly significant ground is that, for many younger philosophers of science of our time, "pluralism" and "perspectivism" are "where it's at," "where the action is." I do not disagree. I am skeptical only when the considerable overlap between the concerns and concepts of pluralism and perspectivism, on the one hand, and the relativism of, say, VCE and SSK, on the other hand, is downplayed or ignored. Fortunately, there are some early signs of a positive and productive rapprochement of all four sides.[262]

There is another area, too, where relativism (in the philosophy of science and SSK) has recently seen something of a comeback. I mean the debate over the causes of contemporary "post-truth politics," that is, a form of politics in which scientific expertise is regularly "trumped" [sic!] by appeals to instinct, emotion, or personal belief. I shall end this Element with a brief reflection on the claim that relativism has generated many arguments and forms of analysis that are used by post-truth thinkers. This claim is the central thesis of the chapter "Did Postmodernism Lead to Post-Truth?" in Lee McIntyre's influential little 2018 book *Post-Truth*.[263] "Post-truth" here comprises "Intelligent Design" (=ID) as well as climate-change denial. And "postmodernism" includes relativism and especially SSK.

McIntyre offers two main pieces of evidence for his thesis: Robert Pennock's "The Postmodern Sin of Intelligent Design Creationism" (from 2010)[264] and Bruno Latour, "Why Has Critique Run Out of Steam?" (from 2004).[265]

---

[261] Daston, "History of Science," 119.

[262] Chang, "Relativism"; Creţu and Massimi (eds.), *Knowledge.*

[263] McIntyre, *Post-Truth*, chapter 6.   [264] Pennock, "Postmodern Sin."

[265] Latour, "Critique."

Relativism and Intelligent Design

Pennock's paper focuses primarily on interviews with C. Philip Johnson, one of the leading figures of the ID movement. Pennock cites a number of passages in which Johnson declares his interest in postmodernism and SSK. Johnson wishes to "deconstruct ... philosophical barriers" to ID, and he sees "relativistic pluralism" as a key tool.[266] Moreover, Johnson presents Darwinism and ID as incommensurable, and attacks evolutionary biologists as a "priesthood."[267] Johnson takes postmodernism to have shown that reasoning is ultimately grounded in "an instinct, or revelation."[268] And in 1990 Johnson complained that "the sociology-of-knowledge approach has not yet been applied to Darwinism." Pennock suggests that Johnson's 1991 book, *Darwin on Trial*, is doing just that.[269]

What does this show? Is Johnson a smoking gun linking relativism to the crime-scene of post-truth? First, note that Johnson's use of postmodernism is highly selective. For instance, he wants nothing to do with postmodernist arguments in defense of LGBT rights.[270] He also worries that postmodernism leads to "nihilism."[271] Pennock himself acknowledges that Johnson's uses of postmodernism are "only tactical."[272] Pennock also relates that other ID theorists oppose postmodern relativism as inimical to Christian belief.[273]

Second, Pennock's analysis is at times a little blinkered. For instance, recall that he takes Johnson's *Darwin on Trial* to be an SSK-study of sort.[274] This is far from clear. None of the central figures, terms, and modes of analysis of SSK (or postmodernism) appear in the book. The central figure of the work – with forty mentions in the text – is Karl Popper. The backbone of Johnson's argument is Popper's one-time (and later recanted) claim that Darwinism is not a scientific theory. Which raises this question: if Johnson's occasional uses of relativism discredit postmodernism and SSK, why don't Johnson's more-than-just-occasional uses of Popper discredit the philosophy of science? Third, Pennock's argument and Johnson's occasional hand-waving in the direction of SSK are ironic given the history of sociology. After all, Durkheim, Simmel, and Weber all wrote extensively about the sociology of religion.[275] And to this day, many theologians denounce such analyses as "relativistic" and "sinful." "*Plus ça change, plus c'est la même chose.*" I conclude that no jury in the world should convict relativism of the crime of aiding and abetting the ID-assault on evolutionary biology.

---

[266] Pennock, "Postmodern Sin," 759–60.   [267] Ibid., 760.   [268] Ibid., 771.   [269] Ibid., 767.
[270] Ibid., 772.   [271] Ibid., 774.   [272] Ibid., 757.   [273] Ibid., 775.   [274] Johnson, *Darwin*.
[275] Durkheim, *Elementary Forms*; Simmel, *Religion*; Weber, *Protestant Ethic*.

Relativism and Science and Technology Studies

McIntyre reads Latour's 2004 paper "Why Has Critique Run Out of Steam?" as a confession: allegedly, Latour here admits that "Science and Technology Studies" (of which SSK is a part) is indeed guilty of having provided post-truth thinkers with their critical tools. Latour starts off by describing his horror when realizing that some climate-change deniers use arguments reminiscent of STS. Latour writes:

> entire Ph.D. programs are still running to make sure that good American kids are learning the hard way that facts are made up, that there is no such thing as natural, unmediated, unbiased access to truth, that we are always prisoners of language, that we always speak from a particular standpoint, and so on, while dangerous extremists are using the very same argument of social construction to destroy hard-won evidence that could save our lives.[276]

McIntyre comments that "one doesn't find a more full-blooded expression of regret in academe than this."[277] I beg to differ. To begin with, Latour's self-flagellation is entirely tongue-in-cheek. As the second half of his paper makes clear enough, his 2004 misgivings about sociology and social critique just repeat criticisms he has been voicing since the late 1980s.[278] In 2004, Latour is not confessing to anything: he is, rather, throwing almost all of sociology and social critique under the bus.

In a nutshell, Latour complains that sociology and social critique have always been stuck in just two modes of analysis. Either sociology studies how humans project their mental states upon external objects (think Durkheim on religion!), or sociology investigates how worldly objects determine mental states (think Marx on ideology!). Both moves are meant to unmask: objects are not as objective as they seem; mental states are not as self-determined as we naïvely assume. Latour claims that climate-change deniers use both modes of analysis. They say that climate change is not a fact but a projection, or that climate science is ideological. Latour's "solution" is to dump the sociological tradition and rely instead upon central motifs in Heidegger and Whitehead.

I have elsewhere explained why I see little merit in Latour's project.[279] SSK-theorists have done likewise.[280] I lack the space to repeat this criticism here. Still, three points seem to me important in the present context. First, if SSK is discredited by the fact that climate-change deniers use some of its tools, why then isn't Latour's project discredited by the fact that the tools of analysis he

---

[276] Latour, "Critique," 227.   [277] McIntyre, *Post-Truth*, loc. 2155.
[278] See e.g. Latour, *We Have Never Been Modern*.
[279] Kusch, "Review of Latour"; Kusch, "Review of Latour and Hacking."
[280] Especially Bloor, "Anti-Latour"; Collins and Yearley, "Epistemological Chicken."

borrows from Heidegger were used by Heidegger to legitimize the Nazi regime? Second, go back to Latour's list of STS sins. I don't think that today one finds many STS-scholars supporting flat-footed claims such as "facts are made up" or (the Heideggerian!) "we are always prisoners of language."[281] Furthermore, I very much doubt that Latour believes in an "unmediated ... access to truth." And the claim "we always speak from a particular standpoint" has both trivially true and silly interpretations.

Third, there is no denying that some climate-science skeptics use modes of analysis first developed in relativistic forms of social theory.[282] I do not think that this fact by itself discredits these forms of social theory. I would rather say that this fact puts the onus on the relativist theorists to explain, preferably to the wider public, how and why the climate-science skeptics' uses of these forms of analysis are mistaken. For instance, SSK-theorists try to understand the social complexity and variability of scientific work. As the SSK case studies aim to show, scientific results emerge out of complex social processes involving data, theories, expectations, needs, values, interests, negotiations ... and many other, further contingencies. SSK takes its case studies to confirm its methodological premise that scientific results are relative in various ways. Still, for SSK, such relativity does not automatically undermine science's cognitive authority. On the contrary, SSK-theorists see no reason to doubt that what results from these social processes in science is typically the best we can at present hope to achieve. Climate-science skeptics take the SSK case studies very differently: they see the contingencies of scientific work as licensing doubt about scientific results. In so doing, climate-science skeptics use as their measuring stick an ideal of science according to which "good" science is not contingent or relative in the mentioned ways. In other words, climate skeptics use SSK work *hypocritically within an absolutist-ideal epistemic framework* – the very framework SSK works so hard to challenge.

Fourth, just as in the case of ID, so also in the case of climate-change deniers: they do not just borrow from SSK, STS, or social theory more broadly. They borrow from all corners of the intellectual world. Indeed, Trump's attack on climate science borrows a lot from traditional images of science, the very image that STS has been challenging.

I conclude that Latour is not a reliable witness when it comes to the thesis that social theory has paved the way for post-truth thinking. Is there perhaps a better witness for the prosecution that McIntyre has overlooked? Would the

---

[281] Heidegger, *Poetry, Language, Thought.*

[282] This is acknowledged by authors in SSK. See Collins, Evans, and Weinel, "STS."

STS-sociologist Steve Fuller perhaps be an incriminating piece of evidence? After all, in his 2018 book *Post-Truth: Knowledge as Power Game*[283] Fuller urges STS to proudly own post-truth thinking. Not to forget that Fuller has defended the right to teach ID in American courtrooms. To assess the suggestion that Fuller is what McIntyre needs, it suffices to take a brief look at *Post-Truth: Knowledge as Power Game*, as well as at Fuller's 2015 study *Knowledge: The Philosophical Quest in History*.[284] The first thing to say on that basis is that Fuller is not a relativist. He calls himself a "left-wing Popperian"[285] and praises Sir Karl as "the most noteworthy if not the greatest philosopher of the twentieth century."[286] Accordingly, Fuller opposes relativism and calls on STS to analyze scientific progress and to develop epistemic and political critiques of science.[287]

Second, Fuller also defends what he calls "the Creationist Left version of ID." Amongst other things, this amounts to taking the "Jesus Stance" on scientific progress, that is, the view that the "total knowledge" and "the eternal life in a perfect state" that "humanity 2.0" will ultimately reach "justif[ies] all the sacrifices that have preceded it." Such "sacrifices" include the "harming [of] many humans in the short or medium term" that "extreme scientists – including Nazi ones" have engaged in. Indeed, Fuller rejects "demonizing" such Nazi scientists as "'pathological', [or] 'inhumane'."[288] In other words, Fuller is against demonizing as inhumane the likes of the Auschwitz doctor Josef Mengele. This is a horrific and dangerous position, which owes nothing to SSK, STS, or Popperian philosophy. And if relativism fails to measure up to the "Jesus Stance," all the better.

Finally, let me make a comment on Fuller's demand that STS should proudly own post-truth. Fuller gives a rather peculiar prehistory of post-truth, a prehistory that starts with Socrates, Plato, and the Sophists and ends with logical positivists and Popperians, Wittgenstein, Latour, and of course Fuller himself.[289] What unites this mixed bag of thinkers is their predilection for so-called "post-truth games": "In a truth game, . . . opponents contest each other according to agreed rules, . . . In a post-truth game, the aim is to defeat your opponent in the full knowledge that the rules of the game might change."[290] This is unconvincing. Sure, Kuhn, Popper, Plato, and the later Wittgenstein – not to forget Trump, Conway, or Johnson – all allow for, or engage in, arguments in which the rules of the game might change. Indeed – but then who doesn't? It makes

---

[283] Fuller, *Post-Truth*.   [284] Fuller, *Knowledge*.   [285] Ibid., loc. 3818.   [286] Ibid., loc. 3336.
[287] Fuller, *Post-Truth*, loc. 4380, 5618.   [288] Fuller, *Knowledge*, loc. 2043–47, 5602.
[289] Fuller, *Post-Truth*, loc. 610, 896, 912, 930, 1267.   [290] Ibid., loc. 87.

a mockery of the whole discussion of post-truth phenomena if a mere disregard for "agreed rules" is a necessary and sufficient condition.

To sum up, Fuller's writings do not establish anything interesting about the relationship between relativism and post-truth. McIntyre must keep searching for a smoking gun.

References

Alston, W. P., "Epistemic Desiderata," *Philosophy and Phenomenological Research* 53 (1993): 527–51.

Andersen, H., P. Barker and X. Chen, *The Cognitive Structure of Scientific Revolutions* (Cambridge: Cambridge University Press, 2006).

Argamakova, A., "Modeling Scientific Development: Lessons from Thomas Kuhn," in Mizrahi (ed.), *Kuhnian Image*, pp. 45–60.

Baghramian, M. and J. A. Carter, "Relativism," *Stanford Encyclopedia of Philosophy* (Winter 2017 edn, plato.stanford.edu/entries/relativism/; accessed January 20, 2020).

Baghramian, M. and A. Coliva, *Relativism* (London: Routledge, 2019).

Barnes, B., "Acceptance: Science Studies and the Empirical Understanding of Science," *Science, Technology & Human Values* 24 (1999): 376–83.

Barnes, B., "Natural Rationality: A Neglected Concept in the Social Sciences," *Philosophy of the Social Sciences* 6 (1976): 115–26.

Barnes, B., "On the Conventional Character of Knowledge and Cognition," *Philosophy of the Social Sciences* 11 (1981): 303–33.

Barnes, B., "Realism, Relativism and Finitism," in D. Raven, L. van Vucht Tijssen and J. de Wolf (eds.), *Cognitive Relativism and Social Science* (New Brunswick, NJ: Transaction Publishers, 1992), pp. 131–47.

Barnes, B., *T.S. Kuhn and Social Science* (London: Macmillan, 1982).

Barnes, B. and D. Bloor, "Relativism, Rationalism and the Sociology of Knowledge," in M. Hollis and S. Lukes (eds.), *Rationality and Relativism* (Oxford: Blackwell, 1982), pp. 21–47.

Beall, J. C. and G. Restall, *Logical Pluralism* (Oxford: Oxford University Press, 2005).

Bellarmine, R., "Letter on Galileo's Theories (1615)," *Modern History Sourcebook* (https://sourcebooks.fordham.edu/mod/1615bellarmine-letter.asp; accessed January 20, 2020).

Biagioli, M., *Galileo, Courtier: The Practice of Science in the Culture of Absolutism* (Chicago, IL: University of Chicago Press, 1993).

Biagioli, M., "The Anthropology of Incommensurability," *Studies in History and Philosophy of Science* 21 (1990): 183–209.

Bird, A., "Incommensurability Naturalized," in Soler, Sankey and Hoyningen-Huene (eds.), *Rethinking Scientific Change*, pp. 21–39.

Bird, A., "Kuhn, Naturalism, and the Social Study of Science," in Kindi and Arabatzis (eds.), *Kuhn's Structure*, pp. 205–30.

Bird, A., *Thomas Kuhn*, (Princeton, MA: Princeton University Press, 2000).

Blackwell, R. J., *Galileo, Bellarmine, and the Bible* (Notre Dame: University of Notre Dame Press, Kindle edition, 1991).

Bloor, D., "Anti-Latour," *Studies in History and Philosophy of Science* 30 (1999): 81–112.

Bloor, D., "Durkheim and Mauss Revisited: Classification and the Sociology of Knowledge," *Studies in History and Philosophy of Science* 13 (1982): 267–97.

Bloor, D., "Epistemic Grace," *Common Knowledge* 12 (2007): 250–80.

Bloor, D., "Epistemology or Psychology," *Studies in the History and Philosophy of Science* 5 (1975): 382–95.

Bloor, D., *Knowledge and Social Imagery*, 2nd edn (Chicago, IL: University of Chicago Press, 1991).

Bloor, D., "Relativism and the Sociology of Scientific Knowledge," in Hales (ed.), *Companion*, pp. 433–55.

Bloor, D., *The Enigma of the Aerofoil: Rival Theories in Aerodynamics, 1909–1930* (Chicago, IL: University of Chicago Press, 2011).

Bloor, D., *Wittgenstein: A Social Theory of Knowledge* (New York: Columbia University Press, 1983).

Bloor, D., *Wittgenstein, Rules and Institutions* (London: Routledge, 1997).

Boghossian, P., "Der Relativismus des Normativen," in M. Gabriel (ed.), *Der Neue Realismus* (Frankfurt am Main: Suhrkamp, 2014), pp. 362–95.

Boghossian, P., *Fear of Knowledge: Against Relativism and Constructivism* (Oxford: Clarendon Press, 2006).

Boghossian, P., "How Are Objective Epistemic Reasons Possible?" *Philosophical Studies* 106 (2001): 1–40.

Boghossian, P., "Three Kinds of Relativism," in Hales (ed.), *Companion*, pp. 53–69.

Briatte, F., "Interview with David Bloor" (halshs.archives-ouvertes.fr/halshs-01511329/file/InterviewDB_FBriatte2007.pdf, 2007, accessed January 15, 2020).

Carnap, R., *The Continuum of Inductive Methods* (Chicago, IL: University of Chicago Press, 1952).

Carnap, R., *The Logical Syntax of Language* (London, Kegan Paul, 1937).

Carter, J. A., *Metaepistemology and Relativism* (Basingstoke: Palgrave Macmillan, 2016).

Chakravartty, A., *Scientific Ontology: Integrating Naturalized Metaphysics and Voluntarist Epistemology* (Oxford: Oxford University Press, 2017).

Chakravartty, A., "Stance Relativism: Empiricism versus Metaphysics," *Studies in History and Philosophy of Science* 34 (2004): 173–84.

Chang, H., *Is Water H$_2$O? Evidence, Realism and Pluralism*, (Berlin: Springer, 2012).

Chang, H., "Relativism," in Kusch (ed.), *Relativism*, pp. 379–87.

Code, L., *Rhetorical Spaces: Essays on Gendered Location* (London: Routledge, 1995).

Collins, H. M., *Gravity's Shadow: The Search for Gravitational Waves* (Chicago, IL: University of Chicago Press, 2004).

Collins, H. M., R. Evans and M. Weinel, "STS as Science or Politics?" *Social Studies of Science* 47 (2007): 580–6.

Collins, H. M. and S. Yearley, "Epistemological Chicken," in Pickering (ed.), *Science*, pp. 343–68.

Craig, E., *Knowledge and the State of Nature* (Oxford: Clarendon Press, 1999).

Creager, A. N. H., "Paradigms and Exemplars Meet Biomedicine," in Richards and Daston (eds.), *Kuhn's* Structure, pp. 151–66.

Crețu, A.-M. and M. Massimi (eds.), *Knowledge from a Human Point of View* (New York: Springer, 2019).

Dancy, J., "Moral Particularism," *Stanford Encyclopedia of Philosophy* (Winter 2017 edn, plato.stanford.edu/entries/moral-particularism/, accessed January 20, 2020).

Daston, L., "History of Science without *Structure*," in Richards and Daston (eds.), *Kuhn's* Structure, 115–32.

Dupre, J., *The Disorder of Things: Metaphysical Foundations of the Disunity of Science* (Cambridge, MA: Harvard University Press, 1995).

Durkheim, E., *The Elementary Forms of the Religious Life*, transl. by K. E. Fields (New York: The Free Press, 1995).

Feyerabend, P., *Against Method: Outline of an Anarchistic Theory of Knowledge* (London: NLB, 1975).

Feyerabend, P., "Classical Empiricism," in Feyerabend, P., *Problems of Empiricism: Philosophical Papers*, 2 vols. (Cambridge: Cambridge University Press, 1981), vol. II, pp. 34–51.

Feyerabend, P., *Conquest of Abundance: A Tale of Abstraction versus the Richness of Being* (Chicago, IL: University of Chicago, 1999).

Field, H., "Epistemology without Metaphysics," *Philosophical Studies* 143 (2009): 249–90.

Finocchiaro, M. A. (2005), *Retrying Galileo, 1633–1992* (Berkeley, CA: University of California Press).

Frank, P., *Wahrheit, relativ oder absolut?* (Zurich: Pan-Verlag, 1952).

Friedman, M., *Dynamics of Reason* (Stanford, CA: CSLI Publications, Kindle edn, 2001).

Friedman, M., "Extending the Dynamics of Reason," *Erkenntnis* 75 (2011): 431–44.

Friedman, M., "On the Sociology of Scientific Knowledge and Its Philosophical Agenda," *Studies in History and Philosophy of Science* 29 (1998): 239–71.

Fuller, S., *Knowledge: The Philosophical Quest in History* (London: Routledge, 2015).

Fuller, S., *Post-Truth: Knowledge as a Power Game* (London: Anthem, Kindle edn, 2018).

Galison, P., "Practice All the Way Down," in Richards and Daston (eds.), *Kuhn's* Structure, pp. 42–70.

Garber, D., "Why the Scientific Revolution Wasn't a Scientific Revolution," in Richards and Daston (eds.), *Kuhn's* Structure, pp. 133–49.

Giere, R., *Scientific Perspectivism* (Chicago, IL: University of Chicago Press, Kindle edn, 2006).

Greene, J. C., "The Kuhnian Paradigm and the Darwinian Revolution in Natural History," in D. H. D. Roller (ed.), *Perspectives in the History of Science and Technology* (Norman: University of Oklahoma Press, 1971), pp. 3–25.

Haack, S., *Manifesto of a Passionate Moderate: Unfashionable Essays* (Chicago, IL: University of Chicago Press, 1998).

Hacking, I., "Introductory Essay," in Kuhn, *Structure*, Kindle loc. 59–522.

Hales, S., "Motivations for Relativism as a Solution to Disagreements," *Philosophy* 89 (2014): 63–82.

Hales, S. (ed.), *The Oxford Companion to Relativism* (Oxford: Wiley-Blackwell, 2011).

Hazlett, A., "Entitlement and Mutually Recognized Reasonable Disagreement," *Episteme* 11 (2014): 1–25.

Heidegger, M., *Poetry, Language, Thought*, transl. by A. Hofstadter (New York: Harper & Row, 1971).

Heilbron, J. L., *Galileo* (Oxford: Oxford University Press, 2010).

Herbert, C., *Victorian Relativity: Radical Thought and Scientific Discovery* (Chicago, IL: Chicago University Press, 2001).

Herrnstein Smith, B., *Practicing Relativism in the Anthropocene: On Science, Belief and the Humanities* (London: Open Humanities Press, 2018).

Hesse, M., *The Structure of Scientific Inference* (London: Macmillan, 1974).

Hoyningen-Huene, P., *Reconstructing Scientific Revolutions: Thomas S. Kuhn's Philosophy of Science* (Chicago: University of Chicago Press, 1993).

Hoyningen-Huene, P., "Thomas Kuhn and the Chemical Revolution," *Foundations of Chemistry* 10 (2008): 101–15.

Husserl, E., *Logical Investigations* (1900), transl. by J. N. Findlay (London: Routledge & Kegan Paul, 1970).

James, W., *The Will to Believe and Human Immortality* (New York: Dover Publications, 1956).

Johnson, P. E., *Darwin on Trial* (Washington, DC: Regnery Publishing, 1991).

Kellert, S. H., H. Longino and C. K. Waters (eds.), *Scientific Pluralism* (Minneapolis, MN: University of Minnesota Press, 2006).

Kindi, V. and T. Arabatzis (eds.), *Kuhn's "The Structure of Scientific Revolutions"* Revisited (New York: Routledge, 2012).

Köhnke, K. C., *The Rise of Neo-Kantianism: German Academic Philosophy between Idealism and Positivism*, transl. by R. J. Hollingdale (Cambridge: Cambridge University Press, 1991).

Kölbel, M., "Faultless Disagreement," *Proceedings of the Aristotelian Society*, N.S. CIV (2004): 53–74.

Kuhn, T. S., *The Essential Tension: Selected Studies in Scientific Tradition and Change* (Chicago, IL: University of Chicago Press, 1977).

Kuhn, T. S., *The Road since Structure: Philosophical Essays, 1970–1993*, ed. J. Conant and J. Haugeland (Chicago, IL: University of Chicago Press, 2000).

Kuhn, T. S., *The Structure of Scientific Revolutions*, 50th edn (Chicago, IL: University of Chicago Press, 2012).

Kusch, M., "A Primer on Relativism," in Kusch (ed.), *Relativism*, pp. 1–7.

Kusch, M., *A Sceptical Guide to Meaning and Rules: Defending Kripke's Wittgenstein* (Chesham: Acumen, 2006).

Kusch, M., "Epistemological Anarchism Meets Epistemic Voluntarism: Feyerabend's *Against Method* and van Fraassen's *The Empirical Stance*," in K. Bschir and J. Shaw (eds.), *Paul Feyerabend* (Cambridge: Cambridge University Press), forthcoming.

Kusch, M., *Psychologism: A Case Study in the Sociology of Scientific Knowledge* (London: Routledge, 1995).

Kusch, M., "Relativism in the Sociology of Scientific Knowledge Revisited", in N. Ashton, M. Kusch, R. McKenna and K. Sodoma (eds.), *Social Epistemology and Epistemic Relativism* (New York and London: Routledge, 2020), pp. 184–203.

Kusch, M., "Relativist Stances, Virtues and Vices", *Proceeding of the Aristotelian Society* XCIII (2019): 271–91.

Kusch, M., "Review of Latour, Pandora's Hope and Hacking, The Social Construction of What?" *Studies in History and Philosophy of Science* A33 (2002): 639–47.

Kusch, M., "Review of Latour, We Have Never Been Modern," *British Journal for the History of Science* 28 (1995): 125–6.

Kusch, M., "Social Epistemology and Scientific Realism," in Saatsi (ed.), *Scientific Realism*, 261–75.

Kusch, M. (ed.), *The Routledge Handbook of Philosophy of Relativism* (London and New York: Routledge, 2020).

Ladyman, J., "The Scientistic Stance: The Empirical and the Materialist Stances Reconciled," *Synthese* 178 (2011): 87–98.

Lange, M., *An Introduction to the Philosophy of Physics* (Oxford: Wiley, 2002).

Lange, M., "Review Essay on *Dynamics of Reason*," *Philosophy and Phenomenological Research* 68 (2004): 702–12.

Latour, B., *We Have Never Been Modern*, transl. by C. Porter (Cambridge, MA: Harvard University Press, 1993).

Latour, B., "Why Has Critique Run out of Steam? From Matters of Facts to Matters of Concern," *Critical Inquiry* 30 (2004): 225–48.

Lexico, "Arbitrary" (www.lexico.com/definition/arbitrary; accessed January 17, 2020).

Longino, H., "Values, Heuristics and the Politics of Knowledge," in D. Howard, J. Kourany and M. Carrier (eds.), *The Challenge of the Social and the Pressure of Practice* (Pittsburgh: University of Pittsburgh Press, 2008), pp. 68–86.

MacFarlane J., "Relativism and Disagreement," *Philosophical Studies* 132 (2007): 17–31.

Massimi, M., "Perspectivism," in Saatsi (ed.), *Scientific Realism*, 164–75.

Massimi, M. and C. D. McCoy (eds.), *Understanding Perspectivism: Scientific Challenges and Methodological Prospects* (London: Routledge, 2020).

Mayr, E., "The Nature of Darwinian Revolution," *Science* 176 (1972): 981–89.

McIntyre, L., *Post-Truth* (Cambridge, MA and London: The MIT Press, Kindle edition, 2018).

McMullin, E., "Rationality and Paradigm Change in Science," in P. Horwich (ed.), *World Changes: Thomas Kuhn and the Nature of Science*. (Cambridge, MA: MIT Press, 1993), 55–78.

Mizrahi, M., "Kuhn's Incommensurability Thesis: What's the Argument?" in Mizrahi (ed.), *Kuhnian Image*, pp. 25–44.

Mizrahi, M. (ed.), *The Kuhnian Image: Time for a Decisive Transformation?* (London, New York: Rowman & Littlefield, 2018).

Newton-Smith, B. (1981), *The Rationality of Science* (London: Routledge, 1981).

Okruhlik, K., "Bas van Fraassen's Philosophy of Science and His Epistemic Voluntarism," *Philosophy Compass* 9 (2014): 653–61.

Okruhlik, K., "Science, Sex, and Pictures: Reflections on van Fraassen's Use of Perspectival Representations," in C. Gao and C. Liu (eds.), *Scientific*

Explanation and Methodology of Science (Singapore: World Scientific, 2014), pp. 156–69.

Patton, L., "Kuhn, Pedagogy, and Practice: A Local Reading of *Structure*," in Mizrahi, *Kuhnian Image*, pp. 113–30.

Pennock, R., "The Postmodern Sin of Intelligent Design Creationism," *Science and Education* 19 (2010): 757–78.

Pickering, A. (ed.), *Science as Practice and Culture* (Chicago, IL: University of Chicago Press, 1992).

Popper, K., *The Logic of Scientific Discovery* (London: Routledge, 1959).

Priest, G., *Doubt Truth to Be a Liar* (Oxford and New York: Oxford University Press, 2005).

Richards, R. J. and L. Daston (eds.), *Kuhn's* Structure of Scientific Revolutions *at Fifty: Reflections on a Science Classic* (Chicago and London: University of Chicago Press, 2016).

Rorty, R., *Philosophy and the Mirror of Nature* (Princeton: Princeton University Press, 1981).

Saatsi, J. (ed.), *The Routledge Handbook of Scientific Realism* (London and New York: Routledge, 2018).

Sankey, H., "The Demise of the Incommensurability Thesis," in Mizrahi, *Kuhnian Image*, pp. 75–91.

Sankey, H., "Witchcraft, Relativism and the Problem of the Criterion," *Erkenntnis* 72 (2010): 1–16.

Scheffler, I., *Science and Subjectivity* (Indianapolis: Hackett, 1982).

Seidel, M., *Epistemic Relativism: A Constructive Critique* (New York: Palgrave Macmillan, 2014).

Seidel M., "Why the Epistemic Relativist Cannot Use the Sceptic's Strategy: A Comment on Sankey," *Studies in History and Philosophy of Science* 44 (2013): 134–9.

Shapin, S., "Here and Everywhere: Sociology of Scientific Knowledge," *Annual Review of Sociology* 21 (1995): 289–321.

Shapin, S., "Homo Phrenologicus: Anthropological Perspectives on an Historical Problem," in B. Barnes and S. Shapin (eds.), *Natural Order: Historical Studies in Scientific Culture* (Beverly Hills, CA: Sage, 1979), pp. 41–71.

Shapin, S., *The Scientific Revolution* (Chicago, IL: University of Chicago Press, 1996).

Simmel, G., *Essays on Religion*, transl. by H. J. Helle (Newhaven: Yale University Press, 2013).

Soler, L., H. Sankey, and P. Hoyningen-Huene (eds.), *Rethinking Scientific Change and Theory Comparison: Stabilities, Ruptures, Incommensurabilities* (Dordrecht: Springer, 2008).

Spiegelberg, H., *The Phenomenological Movement: A Historical Introduction* (The Hague: Nijhoff, 1960).

Street, S., "Evolution and the Normativity of Epistemic Reasons," *Canadian Journal of Philosophy* 35 (2011): 213–48.

Teller, P., "Of Course Idealizations Are Incommensurable," in Soler, Sankey, and Hoyningen-Huene (eds.), *Rethinking Scientific Change*, pp. 247–64.

Timmins, A., "Between History and Philosophy of Science: The Relationship between Kuhn's Black-Body Theory and Structure," *HOPOS* 9 (2019): 371–87.

van Fraassen, B., "On Stance and Rationality," *Synthese* 178 (2011): 155–69.

van Fraassen, B., *Quantum Mechanics: An Empiricist Approach* (Oxford: Oxford University Press, 1991).

van Fraassen, B., "Reply to Chakravartty, Jauernig, and McMullin" (www.princeton.edu/~fraassen/abstract/ReplyAPA-04.pdf, 2004, accessed September 13, 2018).

van Fraassen, B., "Replies," *Philosophical Studies* 121 (2004): 171–92.

van Fraassen, B., *Scientific Representation: Paradoxes of Perspective* (Oxford, New York: Oxford University Press, Kindle edition, 2008).

van Fraassen, B., *The Empirical Stance* (Princeton: Princeton University Press, 2002).

van Fraassen, B., *The Scientific Image* (Oxford: Clarendon Press, Kindle edition, 1980).

Veigl, S., "Testing Scientific Pluralism," unpublished PhD thesis, University of Vienna (2020).

Weber, M., *The Protestant Ethic and the "Spirit" of Capitalism and Other Writings*, transl. by P. Baehr and G. C. Wells (New York: Penguin, 2002).

Wikipedia (2020), *On War* (en.wikipedia.org/wiki/On_War, accessed January 12, 2020).

Williams, B., "The Truth in Relativism," in Williams, *Moral Luck* (Cambridge: Cambridge University Press, 1981), pp. 132–43.

Wittgenstein, L., *Nachlass: The Bergen Electronic Edition* (CD-Rom, Oxford: Oxford University Press, 2000).

Wittgenstein, L., *Philosophical Investigations*, transl. by E. Anscombe (Oxford: Blackwell, 1953).

Wittgenstein, L., *Remarks on the Foundations of Mathematics*, 3rd edn (Oxford: Blackwell, 1978).

Wray, K. B., *Kuhn's Evolutionary Social Epistemology* (Cambridge: Cambridge University Press, Kindle edition, 2011).

Wright, C., "New Age Relativism," *Philosophical Issues* 17 (2006): 262–83.

Acknowledgements

I am most grateful to two anonymous readers, and the series editors, Robert Northcott and Jacob Stegenga. For helpful discussions, I am indebted to Natalie Ashton, Maria Baghramian, Delia Belleri, David Bloor, Hernan Bobadilla, Paul Boghossian, Adam Carter, Hasok Chang, Daniel Cohnitz, Harry Collins, Matteo Collodel, Ana-Maria Crețu, Yuliya Fadeeva, Filippo Ferrari, Mark Fischer, Bas van Fraassen, Sandy Goldberg, Sarah Gore Cortes, Antti Hautamäki, Paul Hoyningen-Huene, Soheil Human, Marja-Liisa Kakkuri-Knuuttila, Jinho Kang, Katherina Kinzel, Anne-Kathrin Koch, Jeff Kochan, Raffael Krismer, Daniel Kuby, Robin McKenna, Velislava Mitova, Sebastiano Moruzzi, Fred A. Muller, Elisabeth Nemeth, Lydia Patton, Herlinde Pauer-Studer, Nicolaj Jang Lee Pedersen, Duncan Pritchard, Stathis Psillos, Irene Rafanell, Matthew Ratcliffe, Pablo Schyfter, Markus Seidel, Jamie Shaw, Katharina Sodoma, Mark Sprevak, Johannes Steizinger, Paul Teller, Karim Thebault, Adam Toon, Sophie Veigl, Alan Weir, Niels Wildschut, Paul Ziche, and Jure Zovko. For research assistance I am grateful to Ernestine Umscheider. – I dedicate this Element to Marietta.

Cambridge Elements ☰

Philosophy of Science

Robert Northcott

Birkbeck, University of London

Robert Northcott is Reader in Philosophy. He began at Birkbeck in the summer of 2011, and in 2017 became Head of Department. Before that, he taught for six years at the University of Missouri-St Louis. He received his PhD from the London School of Economics. Before switching to philosophy, Robert did graduate work in economics, receiving an MSc, and undergraduate work in mathematics and history.

Jacob Stegenga

University of Cambridge

Jacob Stegenga is a Reader in the Department of History and Philosophy of Science at the University of Cambridge. He has published widely on fundamental topics in reasoning and rationality and philosophical problems in medicine and biology. Prior to joining Cambridge he taught in the United States and Canada, and he received his PhD from the University of California San Diego.

About the Series

This series of Elements in Philosophy of Science provides an extensive overview of the themes, topics and debates which constitute the philosophy of science. Distinguished specialists provide an up-to-date summary of the results of current research on their topics, as well as offering their own take on those topics and drawing original conclusions.

Printed in the United States
By Bookmasters